Heads Up!

A Zillion Ways to Survive Negativity in Your Life

Christine Rossi

KENDALL/HUNT PUBLISHING COMPANY
4050 Westmark Drive   Dubuque, Iowa 52002

"Sassy" illustrations courtesy of Kristi Beddow.

A Note from Christine

The intent of my book is to bring hope and love to all who feel fragile when negativity visits. Please appreciate that I share my strong belief in the Almighty lending more than a hand in getting mortal man through tough waters. If I had a magic wand, I would wave it over the world and eliminate all negativity, but the older I become, I realize that the negativity and the manner we choose to deal with the negativity will either cause long-term upset or growth.

This book is dedicated in memory of my mother, Mary. The material in this book came from my heart and that is an extension of the hearts of my grandparents who came to the United States from the Old Country.

A.G.A.H.

Mary Georges
(Mom)

Hoson and Sam Georges
(my grandparents)

When I was young and free and my imagination had no limits, I dreamed of changing the world.

As I grew older and wiser, I discovered the world would not change, so I shortened my sights somewhat and decided to change only my country.

But it, too, seemed immovable.

As I grew into my twilight years, in one last desperate attempt, I settled for changing only my family, those closest to me, but alas, they would have none of it.

And now as I lie on my deathbed, I realize: If I had only changed myself first, then by example I would have changed my family. From their inspiration and encouragement, I would then have been able to better my country and, who knows, I may have even changed the world.

—From the tomb of
an Anglican bishop
in the Crypts of
Westminster Abbey

Contents

About the Author

Christine Rossi is a nationally recognized inspirational speaker. Her reputation as a warm and witty trainer follows her everywhere. The energy she produces infects her audiences with a positive bug. Rumor has it that in the 16 years she has been giving seminars, no one has ever fallen asleep!

Christine has a background in education and business, but her best school has been the University of Life. She has travelled and lived in different areas of the United States and Europe and she always feels at home no matter where she is speaking.

Christine makes everyone feel comfortable and positive in any situation. You can be sure you will get a smile and a helping hand whenever you meet her.

Her priorities are the same ones she teaches: God, family, work, hospice volunteer work and youth ministry. Her sense of style fits wherever she sits, in jeans on the floor with a group of teens, or in a snazzy suit in front of an audience.

This is a lady who Walks Her Talk.

Introduction

How Much Control Do We Really Have Over Our Destiny with Negativity?

"Where am I?" thought Mercedes Ramirez as she lay shivering and confused on a mountain 40 miles north of the Cali airport in Colombia, South America.

Mercedes was on the American Airlines plane that on December 20, 1995, took a wrong turn and crashed into the Andes mountains just 40 miles from the airport. Of the 160 passengers on board, only four survived the crash.

Mercedes had been hurled onto the mountain on the anniversary of her birth 21 years earlier. The gift of life and rebirth once again was granted to her but the lives of both her parents were taken only yards from where she was thrown. Although she was thrust out of the plane around 8:45 p.m., she did not regain consciousness until morning.

When she woke, she could not remember where she was. "My mother always taught me to think of the last thing I did when I lost something, and I had lost a lot of time and could not remember how I got there. It was my birthday and I remembered getting onto the airplane to go see my relatives for the Christmas holidays," said Mercedes.

She began thinking all types of thoughts—of her best friend's weddings she would miss if she died and of her love for her nephew, Nicolis Bullard, who was eight at the time of the crash. She wanted to be there for Nicolis and share his life as he grew up. Love of her friends, of her family, and of life itself got the attention of the Divine intervention that took place on the mountain.

Mercedes tried to stand up, but her leg dangled. She was in excruciating pain and could do nothing but lie back down on the hard and unforgiving rock. She picked up a shiny piece of wreckage and tried to position it so she could signal the helicopter overhead. Eighteen hours later, the rescuers found the survivors and the remains of the plane in the mile-long swath of wreckage.

As she waited, Mercedes began to pray. The helicopters landed and she restlessly waited her turn as other survivors were pulled from the wreckage. The rescuers placed black plastic bags on her for protection from the cold drizzling rain, but all she wanted to do was sleep . . .

The events of our world, of modern society, of daily life in general sometimes hurl us into the dark. The sadness of our own or others' suffering can easily shatter our spirits and our hope. The pain of not being able to move out of a bad situation fast enough can trigger a nose dive into despair, into a downward spiral of increasing negativity.

Negativity comes when we feel out of control, helpless, without hope that anything we do matters.

Mercedes had no other choice but to give up control of the event and put her trust in the doctors and rest her hope in the prayers of the people she knew were interceding for her around the world. Although she knew she could not control the long-enduring and sometimes endless *events* that occurred after the crash, she knew she *could* control her response to them.

Mercedes was in critical condition and intensive care in Colombia when her sister Sylvia went to be with her. Hearing Sylvia's voice in the hospital, Mercedes opened her eyes and communicated through hand signals because of tubes in her throat. She was hospitalized from December until late February and is a real miracle to be living and walking today.

The crash could have turned Mercedes into a bitter, depressed, and impossible person. But the Mercedes I had the honor to interview ten months after the accident was a vivacious, compassionate, and positive young woman, full of hope for her future and open to the path the Lord has for her. She is continuing her education and is a senior studying international studies with a French minor. She surrounds herself with a support system of family and close friends who have felt her every stitch and pre- and post-surgical pain.

"My sister Sylvia's support was so important because she was with me the whole time and I could talk to her. I asked her why God took our parents so fast. And she soothed me by knowing in faith that only God knows and we should not question the

Divine. My parents were very much in love and very close. It would have been so hard for them if they did not die together," Mercedes told me.

Mercedes knows that it could have been intolerable if she had been awake through the entire crash, but mercifully she was rendered unconscious until the light of day. Some of us move unconsciously through the really negative times until the light of wisdom and the process of repair starts. In Mercedes' case, the process was one first of physical repair and healing followed by continuous mental bereavement for her parents and all who lost their lives on that flight.

Reflecting on her own healing process, Mercedes said, "I think we have free will to choose what we do with what happens to us in our lives. I had a choice to be angry, full of bitterness because I loved my family and I miss them, but I choose to be happy and go on with my life in the honor of my parents. I want to finish my education and have a quality life. Some people are full of negativity and should realize it doesn't make life happy for you. The control is in our heart and mind, not in where you are or what happened. Sure, this was hard, it was not easy, but I made it and it is an everyday process. I do not go through a day when I do not see something on television or in the paper that reminds me of the accident, and I feel it. But I have to go on. I know from being on the mountain in the cold, I have a lot I want to do. I am not sure why God spared my life, but I am thankful and open to the world of knowledge that He will lead me to."

Although most of us will never experience the trauma and nightmare of a crash such as the one Mercedes survived, we will, however, experience daily emotional crashes and feelings of negativity and helplessness from situations that we cannot control. In these instances, we must simply learn to trust. The control we have lies in our mental attitude. But as we busy ourselves with exhausting daily comings and goings, we sometimes give up, and may even eventually lose the control over our responses.

Harvard psychologist William James said, "The greatest discovery of my generation is that a human being can alter his life by altering his attitudes of mind."

Do we have more control than we think over negative events in our lives? Does success or failure have anything to do with mental attitude?

In Mercedes and other survivors, the event stopped their normal life patterns, but it did not stop their lives.

There is no escape from reality and the tests of life. Even Jesus cried out to God and asked that His cup pass from him, the prophecy of His crucifixion, while he was in the Garden of Gethsemane. We all have to deal with the realities that come our way. We can accept them, not agree with them. We can change the way we think about them and put them in a special place in our heads. Or, we can leave them and not take any responsibility for them—but then they will still be there.

In the due process of time, all things will settle down or be resolved. We may not be thrilled with the way in which they are resolved, but learning to deal with those moments is part of growing up, of maturing, of coming to terms with our internal selves. When a situation does turn out differently than you expected, do not lose faith. Simply remember that there are bigger plans in the picture for us all. Ivy Baker Priest is quoted as saying "The world is round, and the place which may seem like the end may also be the beginning . . ."

"As Within, So Without"

The Greek poet Hermessianex lived about 400 years before Christ. He left us a four-word phrase that is timeless. He said, "as within, so without." The attitude you possess within will dictate the quality of your outward life.

Consider an experience I had in an airport while I was waiting in a very slow-moving, long line to get my delayed flight rescheduled.

The man in front of me made sure everyone knew exactly how he felt about the delay. He threw his carry-on luggage across the floor, took off his jacket, and started to yell at the customer service representative. There was no answer the airline representative could have offered this man that would console him. As I stood behind him, I remained still, but I was alarmed and surprised at the out-of-control show going on in front of me.

"His behavior was unacceptable, and you did a great job keeping your composure," I said to the representative as I stepped up to the counter.

"Oh, he's that way every time we have a delay," shrugged the clerk. "He's a business flyer who's here every week."

"Why did you treat him so kindly? I would have sent him to the back of the line for punishment," I remarked.

"Why not treat him kindly? I have a full day and a lot of weather delays to deal with. Why should I let him dictate how I'll act?" the totally professional and wise clerk responded.

Obviously, she understood the theory of "as within, so without." We do have control over the way we respond to situations.

The challenge I bring you in this book is to develop new ways to respond to situations and people who are negative. Our lives are fragile. We deserve to live in the light, not always in the dark. We cannot teach others to be positive, but we can give them the tolerance bug through examples. It's easy to catch kindness and to respond positively, but it's also easy to give in to the darker side of ourselves. Which one will benefit yourself and others, to be the wet blanket or to choose to look up at the glory offered?

In every life, there will be pain and trials that we cannot change, but we can learn to change the way we respond to them and emerge stronger people. This book is about that very thought. I have cut four sections for you as emotionally mouth-watering as four big pieces of delicious chocolate cake. Of course, the suggestions I offer are calorie free, but they're full of rich and feel-good ingredients.

The four sections mirror the seasons of the year, for our lives are like the changing seasons, full of birth and renewal and shedding of foliage. But like the daffodils that derive nourishment from their dying leaves at the end of spring to rebloom more brilliantly the following April, so do we embrace the events of our lives—positive and negative—and challenge ourselves to become even stronger, more vibrant people.

Within each section are **"Heads Up!"** suggestions, action steps that only you can commit to for changing your mind-set from negative to positive when faced with your own or others' adversity. You'll also find studies, interviews, and easy, commonsense . . . COMMONSENSE . . . ideas that work.

At the end of each seasonal section are the real therapy steps that are guaranteed to help you bring a balance and zeal to your life. I believe in balance, a little of this and a little of that. You'll find four types of therapies at the conclusion of each section—spiritual therapy, physical therapy, humor therapy, and cooking therapy— that I have created by blending (balancing, if you will) my old country heritage with the modern day.

We all need some support, no matter what season of our lives we are journeying through. No one knows exactly why life takes the turns it does, it just does. It's what we do in the turn that ultimately determines the peace, love, and suffering of our lives. The seasons do not end: they just keep coming, one after the other, year after year. It is our challenge to learn to enjoy the uniqueness of each one. As Mercedes told me, "Now I notice everything a lot more. I notice the sun and the sky and I listen to what children have to say. I had a longing to get back into the swing of life. I had a purpose and a mission and I was not done."

Winter

Shed the Heaviness of Negativity and Experience the Beauty of the World

As long as the Earth remains, there will be springtime and harvest, cold and heat, winter and summer, day and night.
—*Gen. 8:22 TLB*

Winter is the time to chase from your heart all gloomy thoughts and to make glad every day we have.

Depending on where you live, you may have a short winter that lasts just a few months or one that seems to have no end. You cannot escape the attitude of winter even if you are on the beach. Almost all of us will experience a winter in our lives that includes cold, unavoidable realities. This is an equal opportunity time that crosses all gender and age barriers.

The media adds to the excitement with the changing weather reports. The main conversations, no matter where you go, reflect the weather or the anticipation of more severe weather. No matter what the reports are, the mental report card is the one that will see you through. You can have a terrific day doing what you love no matter how severe the storm outdoors, or you can be down in the dumps when the sky is blue and the air is crisp. It is your choice and your challenge.

Mother Nature has her own way of dealing with the times. The animals are pretty darn smart and we can learn a lot from watching them. Squirrels prepare for the upcoming conditions by running around and gathering nuts for their nests. The lazy squirrels are the ones who are out in the snow looking for something to eat, while the wise ones have it all taken care of and are resting comfortably. If we are making plans to be ready for whatever comes our way, we will ease the negativity and stress attached to this time of year.

These are the months that offer us special challenge, high expectations, relatives, a lot of bills, interesting weather, and income tax forms. This is a time of great expectancy and anticipation for something great to happen. For me, the Church comes alive again with the anxiousness of waiting for the coming of the holy night. This is the time to take up the gauntlet and make the "without" congruent with the "within"; in other words, to do a lot of inside work on ourselves. As we step up to the church altar, we begin celebrating the birth of newness and hope. In December, Christians celebrate the birth of their precious Savior, Jesus Christ, while Jewish followers light the magnificent menorah to renew their rich culture, the Festival of Light and remembrance of the Old Testament.

Although winter and its holdings are a time of generosity and celebration, this time of year can also be filled with somberness and more aggravations than we can stand. It is a challenging time because the exterior appears so bleak and this bleakness seems to absorb our very soul. It seems that when negative things happen in winter, they are illuminated during the short dark days. Although this is the ending of a year and the beginning of a new one, the negativity can flow from one year to the next. To get through these bleak times, always keep a picture in your mind of one enjoyable time you had during the winter.

That reminds me of a winter I spent on my horse farm in Kentucky. The farm was surrounded by fifteen hundred acres of rich, well-cultivated fields that yielded corn, wheat, and soy. The winters in Kentucky can be extreme, and the farm house we were renting was also extremely cold. I could see the fields sleeping under nature's blanket of sparkling white snow. This is a time when many of us are forced to be close to one another—or alone with ourselves. I remember playing endless Monopoly games with my daughters in front of the hot fireplace. We would keep the board as we left it and continue the game the following day. It was a good time that we still reflect on when we get together during the holidays. Memories like these can be a bridge to help us over the blues. We can recreate these types of events in our present lives, although it may not be the same game or the same people you play the game with.

Just as remembering a special moment from the past can help carry you through a rough spot in your day, here are some tips for gaining positive momentum on a larger scale. They'll help you refocus from the negativity that may be going on around you to a brighter moment. After all, these little moments make up the hours, and eventually the days and years of your life.

Heads Up! Tips for Gaining Positive Momentum

1. **Get rid of excuses.** When the Spanish explorer Cortez landed at Veracruz, the first thing he did was burn his ships. Then he told his men: "You can either fight or you can die." Burning his ships removed a third alternative: giving up and returning to Spain. Sometimes it takes more creativity to get rid of excuses than it does to come up with a new idea.

   What three factors will make it difficult to reach your objective?

   How can you get rid of these excuses?

2. **Take a whack at it.** You can't change your experience unless you step up to it. You can't make a home run unless you pick up the bat. You can't win the swimming race unless you jump into the pool and let go of the side. What are three ways you can take a whack at moving forward and seeing the negative situation as just one of many events in your life?

3. **Give yourself an "atta boy" or "atta girl."** What have you done well lately? What have you accomplished for others? How many people have you affected in a positive way? What bad things have you overcome? Give yourself some credit and see what you can do to chalk up another pat on the back.

4. **Imagine the way others would handle your situation.** Think of the people you respect for the way they handle negative situations. A manager at your office? a teacher? a parent? a brother or sister? Imagine that one of these people is responsible for helping you feel better about your life. How would they handle it? How would they step up to it?

Am I spending 90 percent of my energy on the problem and 10 percent on the solution?

How can I spend 10 percent of the negative thinking on the problem and the other 90 percent on the solution?

5. **See the solution.** The average mind sees new situations and conditions with a negative bias. When you counteract this natural bias with a positive, more creative mind, you can develop more ways to handle the situation. What are three things that are positive about your situation? What will you learn from the events?

> *"Although the world is full of suffering,*
> *it is full also of the overcoming of it."*
>
> —Helen Keller

Surrounding Yourself with Faith

Do not forget to watch out for good times. To retreat into yourself, frequently meditate on how good God is to you. We often only see what we do not have, or what our children, parents, or spouse do not have. That is so easy to do, especially in winter, when the gray sky contributes to your gray mood. Fix your thoughts on what is true and good and right. Think about things that are lovely, and dwell on the good things in others. That is sometimes a challenge. Thankfulness will bring joy to your heavy heart. To surround yourself with positive people and those who have survived the emotional roller coaster of life will fortify you with faith that you will get through the winter of life. Faith to me is like a warm bowl of Cream of Wheat and a cup of hot chocolate on a windy, cold day. It is always great to know that you are not alone. You have angels sent by the Almighty to warm you. Open your heart and develop faith to keep the fires going even during the tough winter months, no matter how long or short they are.

Have you ever heard the saying, the stronger the wind, the stronger the tree? The experiences of life can either knock us over for a long time or we can be more resilient and snap back. Just how can we withstand the winds of life? With faith, faith, and more faith. A growing number of people are examining their faith and the connection of faith, inner peace, and wellness. *Time* magazine ran a nine-page article in the June 24, 1996, issue targeting the results of studies of faith and healing. Many people are experiencing the positive results from the power of prayer. The documentation simply cannot be denied. Twenty years ago, no self-respecting M.D. dared to relate that the cures of blood disease, heart disease, or cancer could have come from faith and prayer. Modern medicine, combined with the power of prayer, results in spiritual and physical miracles. The spiritual healings are the most important; physical recovery closely follows.

15

According to a 1995 study at Dartmouth, one of the strongest predictors of survival after open-heart surgery is the degree to which patients say they were able to draw strength and comfort from religion.

A survey of thirty years of research on blood pressure shows that churchgoers have lower blood pressure than non-churchgoers.

Other studies have shown that men and women who attend church regularly have half the risk of dying from coronary-artery disease as those who rarely go to church.

Could this mean that prayer and religion have a direct influence on physiology and health? Harvard's Herbert Benson is probably the most persuasive proponent of this view. Benson won international fame in 1975 with the best-selling book *The Relaxation Response.* In it, he showed how patients can successfully win the battle of stress-related ills by practicing a simple form of meditation and prayer.

My personal encounter with the miracles of healing came about two years ago. I want to share the experience because if it happened to me it can happen to anyone. My background is in the Catholic church, and my family practices the faith everyday. That means we live the teachings of the church and realize that the expectations are always a moral challenge to us. But the graces from rising to the challenges are worth the constant work.

My experience with the miracle of healing through the power of God came in October 1995. I attended a special healing mass, encouraged by two faithful girlfriends from my church. I went in pretty blind in many ways, but I came out a much different person.

Father Peter Mary Rookey, a Servite priest with the order of the Servites of Mary, was visiting our area and conducted the mass.

He had just returned from a trip to Africa, one of his many trips all over the world conducting the powerful healing masses. As I walked into the church, I saw Father Rookey kneeling in front of the Altar of Mary, totally concentrating in his prayer. I could have shot off a gun, and it would not have broken his concentration. I could feel the sincerity and love from this special person even before I knew about him.

The healing portion of the mass began, and I approached the altar. I watched as my friends slumped into the waiting arms of the assigned helpers. They all looked like they had taken a good sniff of ether. When Father came to me and blessed me with the holy oil and gently touched my head, a rush of warmth and peace went into me. I too rested in the spirit.

Faith and special healings from the Almighty occur daily, but so many of us are caught up in the day-to-day rush and do not hear anything but the bad news. My life will never be the same as it was before I was touched by the power. Father Rookey is an 80-year-old living saint as far as I am concerned, and he is loved by people worldwide. He moves about the altar with the energy of a 20-year-old. I hear he does up to 400 push-ups every morning.

If we could put his positive Faith and devotion in a bottle, we could all feel that good all the time. But the lesson from it all is that Faith is there for all to touch, and we all come in our own time. I am so ashamed of myself that I did not embrace this earlier in my life, but we cannot go back and change all the happenings. We need to look at what we can do today. This type of Faith makes people get out of wheelchairs and want to live. The peace is what we all are looking for, and yet the hardest thing to obtain. We cannot buy it in the mail, and we cannot take it from others. We can only encourage it in ourselves.

Is Faith Found Only in a Church?

Faith is God's first gift to us. It has many facets and definitions, but it is our response to the events.

During this season, you might try the following suggestions:

1. Set the time for increasing your knowledge of God's revelation.

2. Next, open yourself up to learning from reading encouraging stories about people of great faith who have overcome all odds. There are concentration and prisoner of war camp survivors who have stories that will wake you up.

It always amazes me just how strong we are as human beings. Sometimes we don't give ourselves the credit due during those negative times. We must always increase our faith. When you do this, you will see how hope comes into your situation.

Creating Faith and Hope are very positive ways to overcome the onslaught of negative events.

Do not underestimate the power you innately have—that is the power to use your faith and share your hope. When you spread this type of message, you too will be heading to the top. When you are feeling hopeless, go to your Faith and it will open up the door to hope. Next, put it all into action and you will feel the love and peace come rushing in just like I did that beautiful day in October 1995.

"Ask and it will be given to you; seek and you will find; knock and the door will be opened to you. For everyone who asks, receives; and the one who seeks, finds; and to the one who knocks, the door will be opened. Which one of you would hand his son a stone when he asks for a loaf of bread, or a snake when he asks for a fish?"
—Matthew 7: 7-10

Prayer is a necessary means to help us through the negativity of the world. There is a lack of instruction in prayer. The secret to meaningful prayer is not to repeat mindless prayers that do not have meaning for you personally. There is someone who loves you more than your friends, lover, father, mother, sister, or brother. He has loved you before you were born. Wouldn't you want a relationship with this person and to get to know him better? Well, that is truly the way God loves us all, and we can have a great relationship with Him. Prayer is one way to communicate with God and strengthen our relationship with Him.

When we pray, it is a cry of love back to one who loves us more. It is a conversation with the Almighty. He never interrupts us, and He takes a lot of blame for things that man has made.

Heads Up! Quick Course on How to Pray

1. Preparation for prayer is important. Go to a quiet place. Even turning off the radio in your car can create an atmosphere for prayer. You can pray anywhere, at any time, at work, or at recreation. It simply is lifting your mind to God.

2. Meditation leads to affection and petition. A petition is a request or a special surge of the heart for someone who needs help.

3. The fruits of prayer, according to Saint Alphonsus, are affections, petitions, and resolutions. The end of prayer is uniformity with the will of God.

Some days you will have time to sit maybe for thirty minutes or better, and other days the world will pull you away. Realize that in order to see the results and effects of your prayers, you need to be a bit selfish with your time. Plan prayer into your day. Before you know it, it will be part of your day.

When you're down and need some comfort, try praying. It works better than a hot fudge sundae.

One of my favorite prayers-a real negativity buster-is the prayer of supplication of the Holy Spirit:

> *"Holy Spirit, you who solves all problems, who lights all roads so that I can attain my goal, you who give me the divine gift to forgive and forget all evil against me, and in all instances of my life you are with me. I want to thank you for all things and to confirm again that I never want to be separated from you . . . Amen and Amen.*

> *I asked God for strength, that I might achieve.*
> *I was made weak, that I might learn humbly to obey . . .*
> *I asked for riches, that I might be happy.*
> *I was given weakness, that I might feel the need of God.*
> *I asked for all things, that I might enjoy life.*
> *I was given life, that I might enjoy all things.*
> —Anonymous

December

Patience, Patience, Patience

*T*his is the month to think creatively, act optimistically, and plan carefully.

Just when you thought your cup runneth over with enough to do, the coming of the holidays arrive. Even though they are stressful, they bring good stress. Yes, good stress, and a time to make memories for the rest of the year. Put down the nasties and put the love back into your ever-loving heart.

Here are some suggestions that will help you not only get through the month, but to do so with *total quality assurance.*

Heads Up! Separate Fact from Fiction During the Holiday Season

Let go of unfair expectations on yourself and those you love.

Fiction

1. No one can have the flu, cancer, or heart attacks during the holidays.

2. Everyone will appreciate the time you took choosing their gifts and respond with a thank you card.

3. Your children and grandchildren will take more than five minutes to open the mountain of presents.

4. Your teenagers will have smiles on their faces for the family picture in front of the Christmas tree.

5. All the out-of-town visitors will get along with everyone in the house.

6. Your visiting young adult children will not remind you and everyone within earshot of every mistake you made as a parent.

7. Your husband will buy your gift before Christmas Eve. And you will receive more than one from him.

8. The airlines will be prepared to service the millions of people traveling this time of year and never lose your luggage.

9. You will not receive any sad or bad news during this time.

10. Everyone will be ready for church or temple service on time (and you won't have to stand again in the back for a good hour).

Fact

1. You will get it all finished on time—whatever you are worried about.

2. Christmas is a time for hope, peace, and love.

3. You are more vulnerable to catching colds and flu from lack of sleep this time of year.

4. The holiday commercials are not made with the real theme of the birth of Christ in mind.

5. You do not have to go broke to please everyone.

6. You do need exercise, rest, and time to yourself.

7. You can control the urge to let relatives know what you have been thinking for the last year about them.

8. You can laugh and have joy while carrying on the traditions.

9. You can ask for assistance. Others really want to help out.

10. Your grown children will have kids someday, and they will know that you did a heck of a good job as their parents. (We can hope for that one!)

Beat the Frenzy of the Season

During this time of year we have so much going on. For many companies, it is the end of the year, so everyone is busy getting all the years' information together. On the home front, there are gifts to send, gifts to buy, and great social gatherings. It's enough to make you want to find a cloister convent to escape to. But I'm sure even the cloister nuns and monks have an increase of things to do this month. Yet there's a way to tame the tasks a little and avoid pressuring yourself to the point that you dread the entire season.

Heads Up! December Survival Tactics

1. **Be patient with yourself and realize you cannot be everything to everybody.** You may at times even have to decline from some things you would like to do. You won't lose friends, even if you can't see everyone this season.

2. **Be a bit selfish with your time.** Enjoy those treasured family traditions. Don't cut them short. The reason Americans love to travel to Europe is to experience the old country traditions. Cut out some precious time and recreate the traditions you loved as a child.

3. **Start your own traditions in your home.** After all, they have to start sometime to be passed on from generation to generation.

4. **Be a secret Santa to someone who is struggling.** People in need could live right next door to you.

5. **Listen to a friend or relative who is experiencing loss.** They feel very isolated, especially this time of year, and need a listening ear.

6. **Start a "favorite activity" jar.** If you're just doing everything everyone else wants you to be doing, try this. Take a jar, and have everyone write on strips of paper the things they want to do. Then once a week, have someone pull a piece of paper out of the jar. Everyone needs to respect that request. Maybe you can do this as a family project or as a fun activity to share with your honey. Sooner or later, your request will be drawn.

Beating the Gift-Buying Madness

One of the biggest stressors that leads to negative feelings is the almighty dollar, or lack of it. I am as guilty as anyone this time of year. I go crazy and want to get everyone not just a few things from their wish list, but all the things on their wish list. Once I asked my middle daughter if she remembered what she got for Christmas the year before, and she couldn't remember more than a few things. There is a lesson here. Here is a gift list that will have some lasting meaning—and you won't be afraid to go to your mailbox in January when the bills come.

Heads Up! Gift-Giving with Meaning

1. Give them the gift of time. Make a coupon: "Good for one R & R day to talk, eat, and maybe see a movie or a concert together."

2. Give them tickets to sporting events, concerts, or local classes.

3. Give them memberships to the Sierra Club or the Audubon Society.

4. Give them a coupon that says "Good for one homemade dinner delivered to your door."

5. Give them a tree, a rosebush, or something they can plant and watch grow.

When my older girls were in college, their grandma would send them her homemade oatmeal cookies during exam week. They loved them and looked forward to them every semester. Is there someone you know who could use a lift of some comfort food?

December isn't just about the holidays. It's also about so much to be thankful for. We have just come out of the transitional time of fall, and the sky is telling most of us that it's time to get out the coats and gloves.

Eliminating negativity in any month may mean avoiding situations that will render negative results. We can't avoid all of them, but we can see some of them coming and prepare for them. Let's look at some of them we can deal with head on or avoid altogether.

Heads Up! Avoiding Negativity When We Know It's Coming

1. Avoid contact with personalities who are very difficult. You don't have time to get upset.

2. Avoid buying into others' problems— that friend who refuses to accept any advice and continues behavior that's disagreeable to you.

3. Avoid the thought of changing others. You can have a great effect on them, but you can't change them.

4. Avoid the Superman and Superwoman complex. Insist on cooperation from others.

5. Avoid putting things off that can be taken care of with one phone call. Step up to what needs to be handled and avoid surprises later.

Most of us are doing a pretty darn good job. We need help, though, in relaxing more and not feeling guilty about it. Like a car that's running on empty, we can't go anymore if we don't have gas in our tank. For some, this means keeping the momentum; for others, it means sneaking a twenty-minute nap to reenergize. Our systems are unique, but we all require gas to go forward. Changing your old habits of running on empty will be a challenge for you. Life is shorter than summer vacation—don't neglect yourself.

January

A Whole New Year Ahead – Another Chance

*N*o matter how great or bad last year was, this is a new start, a time to reflect on your wants, needs, and desires. While you're on the run, consider reevaluating your current lifestyle and make a working plan to enrich your next year. January gives you the opportunity to look back and review things you would like to avoid.

Coming to Terms with Change

Re-evaluation and review necessarily involve change. Changes at your job and in other aspects of your life are unavoidable. But what is in your control is better planning for the possibility of a shift.

When the engineers designed the Golden Gate Bridge in San Francisco, they factored in three major forces: the wind, the dead load (weight of the bridge itself), and the live load (the force and weight of the vehicles on it). Keeping these circumstances in mind at the time of design, the engineers implemented expansion joints so the bridge would move with these forces. By designing flexibility into the steel, the engineers ensured that the bridge would move without breaking under the stress.

God created us in the flesh, and we too can withstand a certain amount of stress and negative force. But we need to prepare ourselves with expansion joints to stay flexible. If we aren't taking the factors of our fast-paced life-style into consideration and are trying to hold the weight of the world on our bodies, our bodies will break.

This is a great month to redesign your thinking so you can remain flexible under whatever unavoidable negative stress falls on you. **Blessed are they who are flexible, for they will never bend out of shape.** Remember, you will be stiff soon enough. Loosen up for the next round of life.

How can we better prepare ourselves for whatever the new year brings to our door?

Heads Up! Meeting the New Year with Vigor

1. Know the areas of your life that bring *certainty* to it. Perhaps it is in the area of love, in your spiritual belief, with your work, in your family, or with your friends. Some of these areas will change, but when you feel secure in yourself, the shift won't put you off balance.

2. Know the areas of *variety* that you can enjoy. As much as we like to feel certain, we like also to feel variety. Without some, we can become bored. Lack of variety can also lead to burnout at work and in our relationships.

3. Know the areas of your life you can let God take care of and areas you need to take control of.

Even though we are unique individuals, we all have common basic needs. Eliminating negativity on a deeper level can only happen when we understand those needs. I know that at times when I am being a big "neg-a-brat," it is because I am not feeling very sure of myself. Or perhaps, I am overtired and burned out with my day-to-day life. Once I recognize this, I quit blaming myself and everyone around me. Taking steps forward is easier once you unshackle yourself from the real issue.

"Two basic rules of life are these: (1) change is inevitable and (2) everybody resists change. The only person who likes change is a wet baby," says educator Roy Blitzer.

How do you hold on to security—a basic need—if change is both inevitable and uncontrollable?

Getting Comfortable with Change

Security has to come from within. Circumstances will try their best to take security from you. But like a game of tug of war, you can stand firm and win.

Heads Up! How to Unshackle Yourself and Remain Secure in the Midst of Change

1. **Brush up on your basic computer, organization, and prioritizing skills.** You can always fall back on these important areas no matter what happens.

2. **Brush up on your dealing-with-difficult-people skills.** As the work force gets leaner, the employees are getting a bit meaner. You can always be certain of your response no matter what the response of others is.

3. **Be willing to embrace change.** Fear of the unknown makes us feel uncomfortable with change. Dwelling on unanswered questions and assumptions that are yet unproven is very nonproductive. Take change and what comes with it one step at a time. Leave the **"ya, buts"** out of your conversation.

4. **Brush up on the areas you want to stabilize for the next year and make a plan.** Just doing this helps you feel more in control.

5. **Brush up on those regular get togethers with friends you can count on.** The equation for the pop culture is stress and a frantic pace. This only isolates us at a time when we need more than ever to feel certain about our friendships. We have to schedule the time to nurture our relationships, or it won't happen.

Finding a Secure Place

There are certain places we all go visit to feel comfortable. It's like putting on an old pair of well-stretched-out shoes. No matter how they look, they feel great. We all have places from our past or present where we feel peace and comfort as soon as we know we are heading there. Perhaps it is in a beautiful park or a favorite shopping area. Get back there and touch it again, especially when things are changing in a lot of areas in your life. Sure, you can't go home again as a child, but you can touch on the good memories in an adult way.

For me, it is going home and sitting on the porch of a playhouse my parents built for me as a child. It was large enough to hold at least five kids and a lot of toys. It has windows and electricity. The first thing I do when I go home is go over to the playhouse and look into the window. It's a storage hut now with lots of lawn furniture in it. But for years after I left, it was fixed up for the next generation. I can still see myself as a little carefree kid, with all my dishes, dolls, and friends. If I listen carefully, I can almost hear my mother calling me for dinner.

Where is your comfort place? Is it an old chapel with a big wooden door on it? Is it a family-owned ice cream shop that's been in town for years?

Coping with Forced Changes

Change isn't always good. It's sometimes thrust on us at the wrong time, or at least what seems to be the wrong time. We may be feeling pretty comfortable in our comfort zones, finally feeling certain about our abilities and relationships, and bam!—in comes a new boss, a loved one falls ill, or one of the kids is off and married. We are really more resilient than we give ourselves credit for.

Think of change as adding variety. For some of us stubborn folk, we wouldn't even change our socks if we didn't have to. Change and variety causes growth and produces character. The things that come easy are the most fleeting, but the things that come hard are the ones that are lasting.

For several years now, the business world has been heartless to many loyal and long-time employees. The job they thought they would have until retirement no longer exists. They followed all the rules, did all the right stuff, and they still don't have their jobs. This is an extremely difficult but not impossible change to deal with.

Here are some tips from professional job placement counselors to get you through the transition. Don't forget to pray at this time. You might be very pleased with the results.

Heads Up! Dealing with Job Changes

1. Allow yourself time to feel the loss. Find a professional or a good friend to talk to. Let it out. Then let it go.

2. List all the skills you acquired on that company's time.

3. List all the things you've been wanting to do and putting off. Use this in-between time for a little pleasure. Think of it as a lull before the storm. You *will* be working soon.

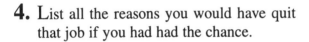

4. List all the reasons you would have quit that job if you had had the chance.

5. List the names of people who can help you find your dream job.

6. List all the things you would do differently next time.

7. List your feelings. You will be naturally affected in all areas of your life. Physically, you may feel tired; mentally, you may be withdrawn; psychologically, you may be short-tempered; and spiritually, you can easily become cynical.

8. Stop beating yourself up with guilt, shame, and bitterness. This will only get you a trip to the nearest hospital or jail cell.

There is a short tale of two monks who were walking to the temple for prayer. They were walking along in silence when they came upon a maiden in distress. She was dressed up for her wedding and could not get over the stream. One of the monks lifted her over the water and put her down on the other side. About a mile later, the other monk said, "Brother, we took a vow not to touch women, and you picked up a woman."

The reply of the monk was, "I put her down a mile ago. Why are you still carrying her?"

How many times have we carried problems needlessly? Move on. Five years from now, or sooner, you may write a thank you note to the person who announced the demise of your old job. It is your choice.

Change can be a fearful thing. You may have to experience a little awkwardness during the learning process. Relax, we've all been there, including you. You made it then, and you'll make it through this change too.

Don't let fear of change keep you from being a risk-taker. Long ago, map makers sketched dragons on maps as a sign to sailors that they would be entering unknown territory at their own risk. Some sailors took this sign literally and were afraid to venture on. Others saw the dragons as a sign of opportunity, a door to virgin territory. Similarly, each of us has a mental map of the world, complete with dragons. Where does fear hold you back? What dragons can you slay?

Heads Up! Take Some Risks to Add Variety to Your Life

1. Learn to play a musical instrument.

2. Ask to be trained at something new at work.

3. Write your memories in a book for the generations after you to read.

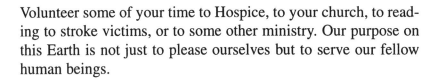

4. Read at least one chapter of a good book every day.

Volunteer some of your time to Hospice, to your church, to reading to stroke victims, or to some other ministry. Our purpose on this Earth is not just to please ourselves but to serve our fellow human beings.

The first month of the year is a great time to feel the excitement of the possibilities waiting for us. It is also the month to make some of those dreams become realities. If you construct a flexible plan, no matter how hardy the wind, you will survive like the Golden Gate Bridge. Plan for flexibility.

February

The Month of Love and All Matters of the Heart

*L*ove means many things to many people. People in love seem to lose their negative attitudes even though events haven't changed. The only thing that has changed is the attitude of someone who is loved and who is loving.

"The cure for all the ills and wrongs, the cares, the sorrows, and the crimes of humanity all lie in the one word 'love.'"
—*Lylia Child*

"Love is to the heart what the summer is to the farmer's year.
It brings to harvest all the loveliest flowers of the soul."
—*Billy Graham*

"Love does not make the world go round.
Love is what makes the ride worthwhile."
—*Franklin P. Jones*

When we fall in love and we are loved, nothing can go wrong. The entire world can shake and quake and you think it is from your last kiss. You never get sick and you are always ready to go. The things that were very important to you suddenly change.

The Greatest Love Stories of All Time

Some of the greatest love stories came from our grandparents and great grandparents who came to the United States from other countries. The journey alone was enough to turn back most, but on they came. One of these stories is of my grandfather and my grandmother. They sacrificed being with their families so they could start a new generation in the United States of America. This was living proof of the love and faith they had.

The very grandparents I am dedicating this book to were an inspiration and school for me. My grandfather was only 14 years old when he came to the United States on a big boat. His home was in a little town by the Holy Land. In the Middle East, there was and still is a split between the Christians and the Moslems. The love and right to practice Orthodoxy was not safe in Syria. He needed to come to America in order to practice his Christian faith. All he had was his dream to hang onto and the love to carry him across miles and miles of water.

As soon as he arrived and was settled, he sent for the love of his life, my grandmother, who was just a kid herself. They started a business and had a family of five children in America. There was never an empty seat at their dinner table as they shared what they had with other relatives who had come to America too. The home was full of relatives, religious leaders, and children. I could feel the love the minute I walked in and was met by my fun-loving cousins.

The relationship between Grandpa and Grandma was too sweet. They spoke broken English, but there is no language barrier when it comes to partnership and living the marriage vows. They were a team, and it was evident in the ways she kept the home and faith when he had to travel during the week to sell rugs and linens. Grandpa passed on to eternity in his late 90s, very peacefully and for no apparent reason. They say that he was just ready to pass on. One year later, my sweet grandmother passed on in the same way, peacefully, from a broken heart. Her partner, her true love, was waiting for her, I am sure.

Their big old house is empty now, but the last time I walked through it I could almost smell the simmering pots of Middle Eastern foods she used to cook. And I could see the many rooms full of loving family. This love between man and woman has carried families through many generations, and will live forever.

A great love story is worth a million violent movies and books. We love naturally. You can witness this through the smiles and eyes of a baby. There are many ways to bring love into your life. Perhaps it is the love of what you do at work that keeps you going. Or perhaps you love doing for others and making a difference. Love truly is the answer. If you could bottle true love, it would be made of the following components.

Heads Up! Love Potion

1. **Loyalty.** No matter how bad things appear, true love can see the rainbow at the end.

2. **Commitment.** Not just interest, but a no-excuse commitment to see it through.

3. **Kindness.** Love is kind, and the actions that go along with it are acts of kindness.

4. **Selflessness.** When you are in love with something or someone, you really do not feel that you are missing a thing. The love a mother has for her baby comes before her needs, gladly. It is a very compassionate and tender love.

5. **Passion.** It is the driving force for love. It may be a passion for the work you do or a passion from the heart for someone earthly or Almighty.

Miracles truly can come from love and faith in the love. This month, reach out and find someone or something to love again. We do not all feel love in the same way, but the ones who only stay as long as the feeling is there are usually just interested. Love goes beyond emotions. It comes from the very soul. Feelings come and go like indigestion, but love comes back again.

Love in the Form of Service to One Another

"The services we render to others is really the rent we pay for our room on this earth. It is obvious that man is himself a traveler, that the purpose of this world is not 'to have and to hold' but to 'give and serve.'"

—*Sir Wilfred T. Grenfell*

The exercise of reaching out and helping others helps us unwrap the negativity we sometimes encircle ourselves in. The tighter we are wrapped, the worse our negativity gets. Reaching out puts life in balance. Think of love as one of the best gifts the Almighty has given you. It will bring peace and healing eventually to the world. It is a chain reaction: service from love and love from service.

Make a list of areas in your life that you feel very significant in.

Heads Up! Unwrap and Reach Out

1. Start a folder of the thank you cards for the activities you are involved in. Reading these feels really good when your world is shaky.

2. Catch yourself doing something kind and enjoy the feeling.

3. Take this month and show your children how much they mean to you. A day just to call your own. Maybe you will have to get them out of school for an "appointment."

4. Let people know in a polite way that you need to hear acknowledgment. Do not assume they know what you need.

5. What can you do this week to make people in your life know how important they are to you? Can you send a note or card or make a call?

Summary of the Season

Winter is a time when you may have to push yourself in the right direction. No matter what the weather report is on the outside, you're in charge of the attitude report on the inside. The busy times of the holidays are never going to be perfect, but they can be a lot of fun. Keeping your sense of humor certainly helps. The preparation and follow through of the new year is exciting, as new opportunities present themselves and we have a fresh chance to make some adjustments for more positive outcomes. Love is the reason for the season, and the purpose for life. We were not created to be hateful, but to love and live in the glory of God the best we can.

Humor Therapy

A man was driving his wife to the store when a policeman pulled him over.

"Why did you pull me over, officer?" asked the driver.

"You were speeding 10 miles over the limit," said the officer.

"That's impossible, sir. I had the car on cruise control," said the man.

Then the wife leaned over and said, "Officer that cruise control hasn't worked since we bought this car."

"I see you don't have your seat belt on either, sir," said the officer.

"I just took if off to get to my driver's license, officer," said the driver.

Then the wife leaned over and told the officer, "Officer, that's not true. I tell him all the time to wear that seat belt."

"Just sit there and shut up," the driver shouted at his wife.

"Ma'am," said the officer, "Does your husband always shout at you like that?"

The wife leaned over and said in a soft voice . . . "Only when he's been drinking, sir."

Exercise Therapy

Unless it is dangerously cold, put on several layers of clothes, gloves, and a hat. Go outside once a day for a walk. The fresh air will elevate your spirit. Walking is always a good exercise. Don't stay out so long that the cold makes you uncomfortable. Promise yourself some warm hot chocolate or tea when you return.

Walking seems to delete negativity from your mind. In order to change our attitudes, we need to change our physical actions. If we sit and wait for our moods to shift, we will have a long wait. But if we shift gears, change scenery, and move forward, our minds let go of the negative event. It will not erase whatever it is that happened; it simply helps us to get our balance back to deal with whatever it was that occurred.

Spiritual Therapy

Spiritual exercises to do to increase your relationship with God.

1. **Turn on the radio and start writing all your blessings. Do not stop until the song stops.**

2. **Write a letter to God and give Him all the people who are stressing you. For example:**

   Dear God,

   I lift up my boss to you. She has a lot of problems in her life and I find it very hard to work with her. Also God please take my difficult mom, whom I can't please.

   Thank you.

Cooking Therapy

I offer you one of my favorite winter recipes. This is a delicious way to eliminate negativity. Maybe it is the process that keeps my mind going forward. All the senses are alerted, the smells, the sounds, the taste, the imagination.

Momma Nicolli's Italian Red Sauce
(a touch of the old tradition that will never change)

Ingredients:

3 cloves garlic
1-13 oz. can tomato sauce
1 small can tomato paste
1-2 tablespoons Italian seasonings (basil, oregano, parsley)
Olive oil, extra virgin (it's easier to digest)
2 lbs. Italian sausage (pork or turkey)
16 oz. rigatoni pasta

I try to use all fresh ingredients. I grow the herbs and can the tomatoes from my garden. I don't butcher the pigs or turkeys—I buy the meat. Cooking is a positive event for me because I usually have a kitchen full of friends, kids, or my husband keeping me company. If they aren't around, I have fun just getting things ready. This is not a gender-specific negativity buster. My Dad used to make the world's greatest salad. My husband does a fabulous linguine and clam sauce. So get your feathers down and put on an apron.

Steps of Action:

- *Turn on Italian opera and try to sing along.*

- *Pour yourself a glass of Italian wine or grape juice.*

Chop your garlic very small. This is a great attitude adjustment. The smell of fresh garlic and the physical ability required to chop the garlic and not lose your fingers will keep your mind on the task.

Take a sip of the wine now and then and keep singing, "When the moon hits your eye like a bigga pizza pie . . ."

Sauté the garlic and herbs in the olive oil and add the sausage. Some people like the sausage in pieces or in links.

Add the tomato sauce and salt to taste.

In a separate bowl, mix the tomato paste with a couple cans of water and add to the sauce.

Pour one cup of wine into the sauce (the sauce likes wine).

Let this beautiful mixture simmer (not boil).

Take several deep breaths to enjoy the spirit of the aroma. This is one of my favorite smells to come home to. I know I am home when I smell the garlic cooking and the sauce simmering. Some people like apple pie aroma; others may like pumpkin pie and turkey smells. The new therapy is accenting the odors we can identify with for relaxation and comfort.

Take some Italian bread and break off a piece to taste the sauce from the pan. It will never taste better than when you dip it in the pan of simmering sauce. Cheer up. Are you feeling better already?

While your water is boiling for the pasta, call a good friend or a family member and let them know you were just thinking about them. What a nice surprise!

Spring

A Time of Renewal,
Hope, and New Life –
A Time of Connection
to God's Creations

Most people need to feel connected to something or someone. Whether or not you're able to affects your ability to experience harmony in your family, on your job, and in your community. Do you remember the handsome actor James Dean, who always played the part of the loner in his movies? As an impressionable teenager, I loved to watch his movies because he was such a good-looking silent island of a man. Little did I know just how difficult it is in the real world for people who are not connected and who believe they are islands standing all by themselves.

March, April, and May are months that offer us special treasures to see, smell, and touch. The miracle of new buds on dead-looking trees and the persistent first flowers that come up every year remind us that it is a time of rebirth. It is a family effort to get all the tulip bulbs in the garden every fall so they'll be ready to burst forth with a brilliant show in the spring. Last year I went crazy at a local nursery and bought the bargain bag of 150 bulbs. My husband was digging the flower bed and I was right behind him putting the bulbs into the holes. Before we covered them up with dirt, I noticed the picture on the bag and the way I planted my bulbs were not the same. I put them all in upside down; they were headed to China. I know that nature has a great memory, but it helps to put the flowers in the right way.

Then the miracle happened, as it happens every spring. The bulbs quietly worked their way to the surface and shot tiny green stems that reached for the sun and developed the bright red tulip flower. Wow! The day I ever take for granted the show of spring, I think I should be cast into the dirt—upside down. This is a time to refresh, to rejoice our minds and hearts. The challenges are still there, but somehow a little easier to handle.

Spring is a time to let the fresh air not only into your home, but into your mind as well. I want to be your assistant in house cleaning this spring, but I want to help you do Spring Cleaning of old attitudes. Time for new life and new ideas to take a new start. Hope "springs" eternal . . .

Heads Up! How to Reignite the Flame of Hope

1. **Expect the unexpected.** Columbus was looking for India. Bell was trying to invent a hearing aid. Colonel Sanders set out to sell his chicken recipe to restaurants. Often what we are looking for leads us to something much different. What are the two most unexpected things that might happen to you this spring? Make a list of five possibilities. The main rule here is not to put four negative things on your list. Keep it optimistic and forward moving.

2. **Revive the ancient Egyptian practice of aromatherapy.** It uses highly fragrant extracts of plants to aid in our healing. Simply walk outside and enjoy the smells of the first lilacs and apple blossoms. Right outside your door is an invisible world, ready to inhale. Did you know that some studies indicate the scent of green apples reduces pain of migraines; mixed floral scents encourage people to buy tennis shoes, and the scents of bananas and peppermint help people lose weight? Feel the smells. Raise your head high as you fill your lungs with new air. Bring some of those comforting smells into your home with candles, sprays, oil beads for your bath, and incense sticks. My favorite is the smell of apple pie, so I seek out the candles and fill the popper with cinnamon and apple. Enjoy!

3. Take time to nourish your soul. Reevaluate your loyalty to belief. If you go outside to admire the first signs of spring with shoulders slumped, your attitude will be slumped also. Change your physical position and watch your mental picture change. Stand like you believe in a good day. Breathe like you believe in a good day. Talk to yourself like you believe in a good day. Say a prayer of thanksgiving for a good day.

4. Make a commitment to take one day a month to do whatever you want to do. Do you remember the movie *Ferris Bueller's Day Off?* Plan something you might plan for your best friend—but plan it for you instead. This can be a day just for contemplative quietness. Or you can do something wild and crazy, even adventurous, like white water rafting. It's totally up to you. This break from your normal pattern will refresh your spirit.

The first time I tried this I found myself thinking of all the things I could do for everyone in my family. It was really tough for me to focus on planning a day just for me, since my day usually includes so many others. So I made an agreement with myself. I would plan a day to go to the art museum and stay in the religious art section as long as I wanted and then have a little lunch in the cafe. Then I would buy a poster or card for my husband or one of my daughters in the gift shop. Another time I took my golf clubs out of the closet and went to the driving range to hit a few buckets of balls. Then I still had part of my day to deal with so I went to the convent nearby and walked on the prayer path and relaxed and had a great day of sport and meditation with my Lord.

It is not easy to take a day for yourself, but like anything that's not easy, the benefit for you and everyone you deal with is worth the time.

ℒet the 𝔈nthusiasm 𝔅ug 𝔅ite 𝒴ou

Everyone is enthusiastic at times. Some of us have enthusiasm for 30 minutes, while others have it for 30 days. Studies show that when we can have it for 30 years, we will have success and quality in our lives.

The word *enthusiasm* comes from the Greek roots *en* and *theos,* meaning "God within." It is a special fire, a passion that burns inside. You can put it on and take it off, depending on the occasion. It can be a way of life for us all. Consider this: It is better to bubble over like a geyser than to be a mud puddle. Who would you rather be around, a person who exudes enthusiasm for life or a pessimistic bore? The majority of people from all walks of life would rather be with the more positive, optimistic, upbeat person. Believe it or not, an optimistic person does not necessarily see events as always working out for the best, but they *accept* that some things won't work out. The positive enthusiasm comes from moving on to the options.

People know immediately whether you're upbeat by the way you walk and the way you talk and the look on your face. Oh, yes, your emotions drive your attitudes right up front. If you're attitude is "not this again" or "Oh no, here he comes," I promise you the person in front of you will know even before your first words come out of your mouth. But if you're wearing a smile on your face, the look on your face will soften your heart. Smiling is actually an exercise. Normal people have eighty facial muscles, and we need to exercise them just as we condition the other muscles in our body. I am very enthusiastic about life. Just being alive and able to do my life's work helps me to stay optimistic. I read an article once that said that professional women won't be taken seriously if they smile and show enthusiasm in the office. What nonsense! I have a hard time not smiling at people whether I'm doing business or in a crowd of strangers. My mom would be so glad she slapped braces on my teeth because I show off those teeth everyday.

Try smiling when you don't want to. The smile will help pull up your mood. *Use those face muscles.* **As Mother Teresa reminds us, "Smile at each other, smile at your wife, smile at your husband, smile at your children, smile at each other—it doesn't matter who it is—and that will help you to grow up in greater love for each other."**

March

Spring Cleaning of Old Attitudes

"It's not so much what happens to us, as what happens in us that counts, or what we think has happened to us."
—W. Clement Stone

*I*f you want to change your attitude, start with changing your behavior. It is not your words that tell others about your sincerity, but the actions you take. It is your follow-through that actually reflects whether there's been an attitude change.

An 88-year-old woman from Kentucky, shares her review of her life in this way:

> *If I had my life to live over, I'd try to make more mistakes next time. I would relax. I would limber up. I would be sillier than I have been this trip.*
>
> *I would take more chances. I would take more trips. I would climb more mountains, swim more rivers, and watch more sunsets. I would eat more ice cream and less beans. I would take one minute at a time instead of living so many years ahead of each day.*

For some of us, wisdom comes when we are terminally ill. Others take seriously the opportunity to make changes throughout their lives.

One of the challenges in changing your attitude is being persistent. You know how safe it is to act in a familiar manner. But when you are sincere about making changes, it is sometimes easier to surround yourself with new friends. Old friends and family are comfortable with the old you and may question your changes. Those who knew you from before will be your toughest critics.

A big reason for my decision to change my attitude came from my near-death experience in 1984. I was a single parent of three and working about 60 hours a week in a high-pressure job. I was pooped. The work seemed to have no end. I had no connection to the city I was living in other than I was one of the hundreds of commuters. I felt no connection to the Church. I only visited it on special occasions and chose to sleep late on Sundays. I had no connection to my family other than providing for them because they were normal self-absorbed teenagers at the time.

In September 1984, I had emergency major surgery on my abdomen. I was very ill at the time. When they say major, they aren't kidding. The operation took all my energy. I was alone in my hospital room a couple of days after the surgery when I felt like I was floating out of my body. I could only compare the feeling to one of deep, deep exhaustion. As I floated, I landed in an area that was bathed in bright white. I remember feeling warmth and peace inside of me. Then I saw my mom and my grandfather who had passed on before me. They smiled, but their arms pushed me back to my hospital bed. It was all so vivid, so real. That experience was the beginning of a real attitude adjustment for me. I knew then that I had a great many years ahead of me and I was being given the chance to make something of them. It also convinced me of the connection we have with eternity.

Heads Up! How to Affirm a New Attitude

1. **Put a lion in your heart.** Will the month of March roar in like a lion? "To fight a bull when you're not scared is nothing," says a well-known bull fighter. "And not to fight a bull when you are scared is nothing. But to fight a bull when you are scared—that is something." What gives you the courage to act on your ideas? What will put a lion in your heart to make the attitude change to get along better with those high-maintenance people you deal with?

2. **Identify who you want to be.** Are you modeling yourself after a character on a television sitcom? Or are you patterning yourself after a family member? Take charge and get focused.

3. **Separate yourself from the event that's causing you to have such an attitude.** When you observe it from a higher level, you get a better perspective. The further away you are from the event, the more clearly you'll see your alternatives.

4. **If your attitude is being dictated by someone else's actions, pray for that person.** Yes, I said pray for that person. It's really hard to stay upset when you're counting blessings for that particular person. Also, ask God to take that person from your gut and heart. Your own sensitivity will keep your insides upset and make it very hard to move forward. Get rid of it as soon as possible.

5. **Don't make an issue out of everything.** Of course, we all have strong opinions on just about everything, from politics to ice cream flavors. When you are asked what your opinion is, give it. But if you're not, just repeat in your head, "It is only talk. It is only talk."

How Do You Cope?

Have you ever dealt with a very negative person who reacts the same way no matter what you do or say?

Keep in mind that there is a big difference between response and reaction. People who normally have a *reactive* attitude are quick; their reactions are driven through emotions. People who *respond* ask questions and get information. There are occasions when it's appropriate to react, and occasions when you should stop and think the situation through. I recommend that if you count to five before taking a stance, you can usually eliminate a negative outcome. Those who fly off the handle usually make a bad landing.

Heads Up! Tips on Controlling Anger

1. Recognize what you look like when you are being defensive.

2. Watch yourself, particularly your body movements and voice.

3. Freeze yourself and sit down to relax.

4. When you feel yourself getting worked up, acknowledge the feeling you are experiencing and name it. Is it fun? Is your feeling and attitude benefiting you or anyone you are dealing with? Ask yourself whether the situation will pass. Will you even remember this situation in five years?

5. Another piece of advice to remember is this: *Don't sweat the small stuff.* Relax. You are already aware of the physical response you get from holding on to a negative attitude and letting it grow inside you. It will eventually attack more than the moment.

Quality responses come from the relaxation response. The following paragraphs offer some exercises for relaxation.

Command different parts of your body to release the tightness. For instance, use mental images to create a cool, blue liquid being poured inside your hot head. As the coolness touches your brain, you can feel the tightness disappear. I use this exercise to release headaches and stress. It's a great way to stop negativity from growing. As soon as you feel yourself becoming defensive, pour the magic coolness in your head. No one knows what's going on behind your eyeballs, but all joy and anger start there.

Refocusing your attention using meditation-like methods will help. You don't have to sit with your legs in a pretzel shape, but you can go to a place away from the person who's the source of your aggravation. Pick a point to focus on. Turn your chair towards a window or a picture. Be conscious of your breathing when you do this exercise. Take three to five deep breaths while you're refocusing. All your answers will come in quietness. Being at peace with yourself is a direct result of finding peace with the Almighty.

When you refocus, the difficult person and the problem don't go away, but when you are kind to yourself and give yourself a break, it's easier to deal with the event. That's the bottom line. Highly spiritual people from different disciplines are in control of themselves no matter what the situation. There is a calmness about them that tells us they are going to be able to accept what is happening. Keep in mind that accepting does not mean agreeing—it means letting it be as it is.

Letting Go

Most of us have very stubborn minds. They just don't want to let go. We keep reminding ourselves of how upset we are, how hurt we feel, and how awful things may be. But you have to take the risk of letting go of these negative thoughts or they will slowly poison your attitude and eventually your life.

We all walk past graves of people we have loved and lost. I think of my own life as if it is on loan to the world and to my family. I did not come with a guarantee that I would live to be one hundred years old. Modern medicine and my sense of purpose will keep me on this earth. Then someone will have to let go of me too. When someone dies, the spirit lives on through the people they have touched. It is the body we miss, the smile and the voice. Don't think you will never have them with you. They are with you, just in a different form. I have experienced loss through long terminal illness of a beautiful mother and cousin. I felt their pain through it all. I also lost a friend who died quickly in a scuba diving accident. I did not like either way. The longer illness allowed us to clean up things and prepare ourselves, but it was torture for us all to watch them go through the process of dying. And the shock of the friend I dropped off at the airport and then the news two days later that he was gone left me very empty. Dying is very hard. It takes time for the living to go forward. Tears are the gift God gave us to heal with. **A friend of mine once said that if we did not have tears to help us heal, we would be like ducks flying up-side-down—we would quack up.**

Heads Up! Aids for "Letting Go"

1. **Give yourself time.** Your friends will want to put a Band-Aid on you and fix you up right away. This is more harmful than good. Be consoled by this thought: Pain *does* subside with time. Don't let anyone rush you.

2. **Slowly add excursions to your life.** Make yourself get out of seclusion a little at a time. Make sure you will feel comfortable in that environment. For instance, if you are not ready for a group of people who are loud and cheering, then go to the museum or to the park. Just change the scenery slowly.

3. **Acknowledge the many questions that come from your conversation with others and with yourself.** Our first reaction to pain is anger. We question the event: "How could they do that?" "Who would be so awful?" "How can I go on?"

There really are no answers that will make us feel better, but the ones we give ourselves are a defensive coverup for the pain. There are evil people sharing this world with us. They do not have remorse for their actions against others. The answer to the question of "How could they do that" is simply "they did it." And we need to deal with the results.

4. **Get to the present as soon as possible.** Sit quietly, process the crisis, and ask God for wisdom and guidance. Make a plan in your head and do what has to be done to go slowly forward.

5. **Choose what you are going to do with the situation at hand.** If you lose your job, lose a child, lose a girlfriend, or lose a favorite pet, the shock can be the same. Gold is purified through fire, but that's not easy to deal with when you're in the middle of the fire. Having people tell you that good things come from bad things does not help either. You need to get farther away from the pain to see that you made it through. Even though you did not want it to happen, you will make it through.

Here's a prayer I turn to often when I feel my faith being tested:

In you, O Lord, I take refuge.
Let me never be put to shame.
In your justice rescue me,
Incline your ear to me.
Make haste to deliver me
Be my rock of refuge
A stronghold to give me safety.
—Psalm 31

April

The Month to Be Foolish

*T*his is a month that starts with April Fool's Day, a day on which many of us have some fun trying to trick others. Why not have fun the whole month? Declare April the month for laughter and lightness. Keeping your sense of humor is essential in handling the rapid-fire events that come your way.

Quick: If April showers bring May flowers, what do Mayflowers bring? . . . Pilgrims. (It gets worse. Read on.)

I saw a poster once that said, "Life is a test. It is only a test. If it were anything but a test, it would have had a book of instructions."

Today we seem to be stretching ourselves more and more. But you can't possibly enjoy anything when you're rushing from one event to the next. Lighten up. This is the month to take steps for developing your own sense of humor as well as appreciating the humor all around you.

As Erma Bombeck said, "We sing make a joyful noise unto the Lord while our faces reflect the sadness of one who has just buried a rich aunt who left everything to her pregnant hamster."

Heads Up! Steps for Getting Over the Grumpy Days

1. **Give yourself permission to have a bad day.** Warn people that you just need some space. Wear a button, or make a sign and let people know.

2. **Cope with the blues.** First, write down what's bothering you. Then tell somebody: a friend, your priest, your spouse. Finally, squeeze the paper into a ball and throw it away. It feels so good to toss the blues away.

3. **Make a joy list.** Write down about fifty things that make you feel better. Do not stop with one thing. Fill your day with some of the things on your list.

4. **Connect with a fun person.** Spend time with someone who won't take everything you say as though it's etched in stone.

"A person who possesses the gift of hearty laughter will not be burdened by constipation."

—*Anonymous*

5. **Find babies to watch.** They will make you smile even if you're the toughest nut to crack. Preschoolers laugh 450 times a day (not always appropriately, I'm sure). Adults laugh an average of 15 times a day. No wonder kids don't want to grow up.

At my age, it would be easier to lose 30 pounds than to snap out of a bad day. A bad day is an equal opportunity employer. It has no bias as to gender, race, age, or country. Enjoy your bad day and work on getting some enjoyment from the day. I call these "little saves." Do things like taking a walk in the park or a drive through a special neighborhood that looks like fantasyland. Go window shopping. **One definition of success is this: how high you bounce when you hit the bottom.**

We can only control so much. Then we need to give it up. Here's a moment of humor I choose to remember when things get too thick (remembering it will help you "sleep better"):

> *Momma Nicolli and her husband were in bed about 4 a.m. Mr. Nicolli was tossing and turning and tossing and turning. Momma said, "My gooda husband, what's a matter with you?"*
>
> *"Oh, I owe $500 to Mrs. Rossi tomorrow and I can no pay her back."*
>
> *So Momma Nicolli got out of bed, went to the phone and called Mrs. Rossi. "Mrs. Rossi, my gooda husband owes you $500 tomorrow and he can no pay you back."*
>
> *Then she got back into bed and told her husband, "My gooda husband, go to sleep. It is her problem now."*

One of the tricks to eliminating negativity is simply knowing when to let it go and move on. Losing sleep over a situation is not going to solve anything. Yet when I ask people whether they waken between the hours of 3 a.m. and 4 a.m., nearly two-thirds say they do. Shakespeare said it so eloquently: "The troops invade just before dawn."

Heads Up! Finding Balance

Here are suggestions for things to do to keep busy and help get your mind in balance. April offers a variety of things to do.

1. **Plant something, anything, so long as it is going to grow in dirt.** I prefer to plant flowers from seed, or a few herbs or vegetables. If you live in a city, planters are available for window gardening or flower box gardening. I find it very difficult to stay upset when I am in my garden.

2. **Find something to repaint.** A fresh coat of spray paint makes everything look great for the spring. When I decide to do this, I grab baskets, outside chairs, picnic tables. Be careful not to paint the dog or kids.

3. **Clean out the junk drawers in your kitchen and den.** It's like Christmas for me when I do this. Wow! I didn't realize how many batteries and nail files I had hidden.

4. **Get into a closet cleaning frenzy.** Lock your bedroom door and turn on the radio to a lively station. Then make the commitment to toss those jeans that you will never get into again. We all have them. I have to throw my husband's "too tight" stuff out because he will never believe he's any bigger than the day I met him. (I'm sure the radon or lack of light in the closet causes these things to shrink.)

5. **Buy some new music.** It can set the mood for your day. We all like music that compliments our identities. So the music you bought a few years ago may not be the music that will uplift you today.

6. Get your derrière off the couch and your whole body will follow it. You know what I mean. Get out and smell the roses and take a walk. Grab a couple of soup cans for weights. I don't recommend a head set—you need to be aware of what's going on around you.

7. Wax your car. This is a great time of year to get a coat of shiny stuff on your car. The first time I waxed a car, I could not move my arm for a week, but my car looked great.

8. Find a patch of grass and lay down and watch the clouds. I think I saw heaven one day. My imagination can make all kinds of things from what I see. We are so busy getting places, we miss the great show. The message for peace will come from "up there," so look up and enjoy the heavens.

9. Make or buy special food and go on a picnic. Better yet, surprise someone and take them with you. It can be a kid, a sweetie, or a person who is alone. I love peanut butter and jelly sandwiches, fruit, cookies, and orange drink for a picnic. It brings up great memories of safe, loving backyard picnics with my sister when I was about seven years old.

Celebrate April. It's the month of the new life. A time of hope eternal for Christians, the Resurrection of Jesus. For Jewish believers, it is a time of Passover, where they also shared hope and new life in the escape to the Promised Land. We can celebrate the new life of the resurrection in the fresh air, new colts in the fields, and baby birds chirping in their nests. April is a great month—a month to be foolish and light and grateful for Life.

May

Time to See Beauty and to Appreciate the Gift of Light and the Promise of Newness

This is a month that brings us more light during the day and longer days to enjoy life. As the days brighten, so should our attitudes. But for some, the shadows of negativity are all we see. The reasons are different for each one, but the negativity is keeping our backs to the sun. Living our life in the shadows eliminates all truth. The light is present, if we have the courage to turn our eyes to the light and see the truth. When we are in shadows, we cannot feel the warmth and love of the light. Are we just too consumed with the negativity around us to get out of the shadow?

With the pureness of the month, so is our search for inward truth. All answers come from within. Nothing from the outside will set you free from the cold and darkness. What beliefs benefit you enough to get you into the light?

Heads Up! Stepping Out of the Shadows

1. Realize there will always be good and evil on Earth. Focus on the good, and the good will be attracted to you.

2. Nourish yourself with a good support system. I once read that the reason gypsies have a good health record is the role the family plays in establishing a positive health environment. When a gypsy gets sick, it's not uncommon for six or eight other gypsies to accompany her to the doctor. Such family participation provides not only a support system for the ill member, it also creates a high expectancy for getting well.

3. Choose others who are light-hearted. You can pick carefully your friends and even your family. Some of your family and friends may be very negative, and others may be very positive. Call the positive ones first and regularly, and contact the negative ones occasionally.

4. Talk to wise, normal people. Sometimes older people can have the answer you've been looking for because they have common sense.

5. The light may be found in the wisdom of our elders. *This reminds me of a story I heard about a 67-year-old man who called the doctor's office for an annual check up. "I'm getting married Saturday," said the man, "and I want to make sure I am in great physical condition."*

"At your age, choosing to get married is truly honorable," the doctor said. "You are in great health, and God willing, you and your bride will have many happy years together. Did your father die at an old age?" "Did I say my father died? My father is 86 years old and in super condition."

"That's great! What about your grandfather? Did he die at an old age?"

"Did I say my grandfather died? He is now 105 and is getting married the same day I am. We are having a double-ring ceremony. In fact, his son, my father, is going to be the best man for both of us."

"That is absolutely amazing," responded the doctor, "105 years old and he chose to get married!"

A smile appeared on the face of the groom-to-be as he said, "Did I say he chose to get married?"

Never think people are too old. We are only as old as our negativity allows us to be.

6. **Empower yourself with a purpose.** This means to give yourself strength from within yourself. Many people search for empowerment from material goods, yet Osceola McCarty found another way.

A story about this incredible woman appeared in a January 1996 issue of *The New York Times.* She never married, never had children, and never learned to drive because there was never any place she wanted to go. She dropped out of school in the sixth grade to go to work. All she did was work, taking in other people's laundry and making them look good for the parties they went to. She was paid in dollar bills. She saved $150,000 and gave it away to the University of Southern Mississippi at Hattiesburg. "I wanted to share my wealth with the children. I never minded work, but I was always so busy. Maybe I can make it so the children don't have to work like I did," she said.

Her only valued possession is a tattered Bible and the wish to attend the graduation of the person who received the scholarship she endowed. She does not want a building named after her or a statue in her honor. She would like to empower other black youth to continue their education.

𝓤nderstanding the 𝓒onnection 𝓑etween the 𝓕oods 𝓨ou 𝓔at and 𝓨our 𝓜oods

1. **Power foods.** Eat these when you need to function and respond in times of stress.

   One cup of broccoli contains as much calcium as milk. It also has anticancer properties, beta-carotene, and fiber. Calcium is nature's tranquilizer.

   According to the U.S.D.A., apples contain boron, a mineral that is a powerful brain stimulant. Munch on one to change your focus.

   Yogurt may prevent yeast infections. It is also an anti-cancer food and aids digestion. It is rich in calcium as well.

   As far as healthy diets are concerned, the Middle Eastern diet is one of the healthiest ever studied. It consists of fresh vegetables and lots of natural fiber.

2. Comfort foods. Of course, we seek comfort foods in addition to those that give us energy. But timing is very important here. You don't want to splurge on comfort foods when you're about to tackle an energy-intensive activity. Comfort food is special food for times when you are relaxed. Once the rat race settles down, pull your chair into the "death by chocolate bar" position, and go for it. Chocolate is one of the most popular comfort foods in the United States. Chicken soup and crackers as well as tomato soup and a grilled cheese sandwich are big favorites too. Don't overlook fresh fruit as a healthful comfort food either.

There are many comfort foods, as many as there are brands of soup in the grocery store aisle. You may have your own memories attached to many of them. Don't forget to be good to yourself and treat yourself to some once in a while.

Many of us watch our calories as we choose our foods. I have a list that is fat free—you don't have to pay for the fat.

1. Food that you eat on the run. Calories don't have a chance to attach themselves to you at that fast pace.

2. Food that you eat over the kitchen sink. Gravity pulls the calories out your feet. Check under the kitchen rug—it may be getting heavy.

3. Food that you eat at commercial breaks while watching videos. The calories go straight to the television.

4. **Food that you eat on your way home from church.** This is a sacred law of church-goers—you have four hours that are exempt from calories.

5. **Food your grandma cooks for you over the holidays.** This is good stuff that goes to your soul.

As a general rule, try not to eat with people who upset you. This can cause digestive problems.

Humor Therapy

"There are three rules for creating humor,
but unfortunately no one knows what they are."
—*Laurence Peter*

In 1992, Pope John Paul II left the Cathedral and walked down the many steps to his waiting limousine.

"Your Holiness, your car is waiting," said the chauffeur as he opened the back door.

"Son," said the Pope, "I want to drive today. I haven't driven in years."

"Your Holiness, anything you wish," said the confused chauffeur as he helped the Pope into the driver's seat and got into the back of the limo.

Well, the Pope was driving very fast through the streets of Rome when a police car forced the limo to the side of the road. As the policeman looked into the limo, he saw it was the Pope driving.

"Your Holiness, it is you," said the policeman. And he ran back to his police car and radioed into his boss.

"Boss," he said, "we have a really important one here!!"

The boss replied, "Is he more important than the vice president?"

"Yes, boss," said the policeman. "He is more important than the vice president.

"Is he more important than the president?" asked the boss.

"Yes, he is more important than the president. He is so important the *Pope* is his chauffeur."

Humor and depression are incompatible. Except in severe cases, humor relieves the grip of depression. Even bad humor is better than no humor.

Spring

Exercise Therapy

Spring is a season that offers many outdoor activities. One of the most popular exercises this time of year is gardening. It is an activity that has no barriers. People of every age, gender, and culture can enjoy this fun. It is truly a multilingual activity. When I lived in Germany, I did not speak the language very well. But the garden was a bringing together of all the neighbors helping me and offering old-fashioned pointers that extended beyond the boundaries of language. It was a delicious and beautiful way of making new friends. Just garden—flowers or vegetables, whatever your fancy. I recommend planting herbs, either in pots or in the ground. They smell fabulous and are easy to grow. Digging in the ground or putting planter boxes together with color and different types of flowers exercises your imagination and your body. I still get on my hands and knees to turn the ground around my young vegetables very carefully with my garden tools. But don't stop there. Go get a tree to plant, or a grape vine. The grapes are wonderful, and who knows—maybe you'll end up making wine in your cellar.

Enjoy your outside work with song and an awareness of all the spring sounds and smells. I'm sure those of you with allergies can't appreciate this. If that's the case, I recommend cultivating an indoor window-type of garden. For those of you who are bedridden, have someone buy you a little window plant that will bloom for your enjoyment.

Spiritual Therapy

A story is told about the famed Zumbrati who walked a tightrope across Niagara Falls. Conditions were less than perfect. It was a windy day and the performer was thankful to have made it safely across.

One of those waiting to congratulate him was a man with a wheelbarrow. "I believe that you could walk across pushing this wheelbarrow," the man told him.

Zumbrati shook his head and said he felt fortunate to have accomplished the feat without a wheelbarrow.

The man urged him to try "I believe that you can do it," he said.

The aerialist graciously declined, but the man kept after him.

Finally, the performer said, "You really do believe in me, don't you?"

"Oh, I do," the man assured him.

"Okay," Zumbrati replied. "Get into the wheelbarrow."

If you really believe . . . get in the wheelbarrow. Cast off your concerns, doubts, fears, and self-imposed limitations.

One of my favorite prayers I murmur at any given time is the *Prayer of St. Francis:*

Lord, make me an instrument of your peace.

Where there is hatred, let me sow love.

Where there is injury, pardon.

Where there is doubt, faith.

Where there is despair, hope.

Where there is darkness, light.

Where there is sadness, joy.

O Divine Master, grant that I may not so much seek

To be consoled as to console.

To be understood as to understand.

To be loved as to love.

For it is in giving that we receive.

It is in pardoning that we are pardoned.

It is in dying that we are born to eternal life.

Cooking Therapy

I want to share with you one of the world's greatest energy foods ever! This particular dish can eliminate negativity through the making of the dish—and definitely through eating it. Knowing that you have some waiting for you in the refrigerator can give your day a lift.

Grandma George's Jabooly (Suff-Soof)

My recipe for winter was representative of the Italian side of our home. This recipe goes way back to my Middle Eastern roots. The music you listen to and the outfit you wear has to change too. Mentally, you need to get ready. I wear a black dress with huge flowers on it when I cook from my Middle Eastern heritage. It is rather hard to cook with the veil over my face, so I just use a napkin. No shoes are allowed when you make this dish—you must dress strictly old country. The music needs to have a lot of drums and mandolins in it, preferably someone singing in Arabic. This music is very popular with people who enjoy different cultures. You can find it in your music store in the "very different" section. Years ago there was a movie and stage play called *Zorba, the Greek* that has a great music track. That will work. Music motivates us to do whatever is playing. And the *Zorba* music will definitely get you dancing around the kitchen in your bare feet, twirling a napkin. Go ahead, get on the kitchen counter and dance around a little. Get into it. When I was visiting Athens, Greece, I went to a local restaurant and I was very surprised that the man next to me threw his plate at the fireplace after he finished his dinner. When it broke, everyone applauded. Then many others followed as they finished their meal. It was a sign they were pleased. Hey, when in Greece . . . This is no doubt a stress buster and a plate buster too.

Ingredients:

1 cup wheat (bulgur, a fine grain found in ethnic stores
or health food stores)
2 large bunches parsley
1 cup mint leaves (fresh or 1 tbsp. dried)
1 bunch of green onions
5 tomatoes
juice of 3 lemons
1/4 cup olive oil
salt and pepper to taste

Get a plastic bowl and just to get in the swing of things, toss it at your refrigerator. That really does get you in the mood. Singing to Zorba is easier than operas. There are no real words . . . DA DA DA DADA DADA. DA DA DA DADADA . . . DA DA DA DA DA DA DADA DADA. Don't forget the napkin dance as you take all the vegetables to the sink for a cold water bath (not your bath, the vegetables get the bath).

Chop everything very small and then chop it smaller yet. Use the whole green onion, but do not use the stem of the parsley.

Wash and soak the wheat for 10 minutes. Squeeze the water from the wheat and add it to the vegetables.

Toss another plastic dish and shake your hips a little.

In a separate bowl, mix your dressing and stir it with a spoon. Then put the dressing over the salad just before serving. Add salt and pepper. This is so great!!

Serve with pita bread or with any bread that has a crust.

This dish is worth singing about, so try wailing like the old timers do. It must release negativity because the old timers are called old timers because they are very old. Sometimes the Middle Easterners will call one of the old timers to sit in the back of a funeral and have them wail really loud. It does scare the bageebies out of kids. But I'm sure all the evil spirits are scared away. Everybody is scared away.

Summary of the Season

Spring is a time of inspiration, a time to clean out the old attitudes and practice the renewal of the person. Spring events bring people together in better moods, possibly from the addition of more light in our lives. We can use all our senses: smell, taste, touch, and hearing to enjoy the radiant events of the season.

Faith is restored and your fantastic adventure in trusting Him, of getting into the wheelbarrow, will change your course in life.

It is the time of Hope for new life and life eternal. Everyone looks forward to spring. It is the time of birth—of baby animals in the farm fields and the hatching of the tiny birds. When difficult times happen during this time, your mental attitude is stronger.

The steps of action for spring take us into the months of summer and a continuation of celebration of life and the elimination of negativity.

Spring offers a quieter time than the holidays and a quieter time than the summer vacations. We will dance our way into June, July, and August with flowers in our teeth.

Summer

It's Sum, Sum, Summertime and the Living Gets Easy . . . or Does It?

The season starts out so fun—the sun warms our soul and gives us something great to look forward to. Sitting at a pool, going to the lake, a little tennis in the evenings. Oh, the clanging of ice cubes in a tall cool glass of lemonade. But who has time to do any of this?

Some of the joys of summer can turn negative as you wait in long traffic jams due to road repairs on normally smooth-running freeways. Along with the temperatures rising, tempers can also rise. More crime happens in hotter weather because more people are outside. Daily aggravations can push the calmest personality to the limit when the humidity is high. Animals get crazy as the barometer rises and a big storm moves through the area. The pressure increases, no doubt about it.

Families pack into the car for long, hot road trips that stretch the family budget to the max. These trips aren't exactly like those in the movies, with the kids singing verses of "Row, Row, Row Your Boat" from the back seat of the car. My kids used to get car sick from sitting in the sun. By the time we got to our destination, I wasn't looking too great. I'd spend hundreds of miles taking care of sick kids and pulling ice cream cones out of my hair.

For some who are in business, sales are down in the summer because people are on vacation. That also means that many businesses experience staff shortages. As the summer force is leaner, the rest of the team is meaner.

We have several options for overcoming negativity during this time of year. Again it starts from within. As the sun is shining, so will be our new, bright strategies for getting along with difficult personalities and through sticky situations.

In this section, you will also explore ways to eliminate negativity through your communication style. As the beans grow in the fields, you will grow in spirit and love. The need for growth is as important for balance in our lives as water is for growth of vegetation in our gardens.

If we don't grow, we are not really living. Growth demands a temporary surrender of being safe.

June

Dealing with Difficult People

Scott Love says, "Only the most foolish of mice would hide in a cat's ear, but only the wisest of cats would think to look there."

The point?

Don't miss the obvious. What's the most obvious thing you can do to overcome negativity in relationships?

I have always believed that if everyone were easy to get along with, always smiling, and never cranky, the world would be a much better place. But I'm not always like that. I sometimes get tired and irritable and just want to go hide out. Do you?

The first part of getting along with difficult people is to recognize our own weak areas. Maybe you will recognize a pattern of personalities and situations that are hard for you to respond optimistically to.

Heads Up! Getting Along with Everyone–Even Difficult People

1. Everyone has problems. No one is problem-free all the time. Some of us carry our problems well hidden; others wear them on their foreheads.

2. Our natural instinct is to identify with our own experiences and stories. When another is speaking, we listen for commonality. Maybe the person you are talking with is upset with their spouse about the same thing your spouse did to you. You have a bond. But if that person has nothing in common with you, the tendency is to shut down the "understanding zone" of your brain.

3. Everyone has the basic needs of certainty, variety, connection, significance, growth, and contribution. If the person is consistently difficult, step back and evaluate what's really going on. Maybe that person doesn't feel significant in the family or at work.

4. People don't want to be told how to live their lives. If your advice is asked for, then offer it very carefully.

5. When you get upset with people, the upset can get in the way of loving them. There is something about almost everyone that is lovable. Try to find it.

CHILL OUT. Making an issue of everything others say is not the way to get along with them. Stay calm, and take up the challenge for growth. Successful leaders recognize the difference in personalities among the people on their staff. A key to getting along with people is giving them permission to be as they are. When you mentally give them permission, you take off your back the huge responsibility of changing the world. If someone is abusing you verbally, however, don't give your permission for the person to continue this unacceptable behavior. Consider the source and the circumstances.

Eleanor Roosevelt once said, **"No one can make you feel inferior without your consent."** That goes for becoming angry too.

Heads Up! Keeping a Cool Head in a Hot Time

1. Clean your home, apartment, or desk, depending on where you feel the emotional combustion starting. Take out the dust rag, open the junk drawer, and pull the trash can over to throw out the unnecessary junk. Reshuffle the papers, and sweep out the anger. Refocusing your attention is a challenge. Try it.

2. If you are dealing with people who upset you on a daily basis, be aware of what you eat. What goes into your mouth will affect what comes out of your mouth. For instance, caffeine has a direct effect on your nervous system. Junk food has a direct effect on your energy. A good stiff drink may be calming at the time, but alcohol can also cause you to become more aggressive rather than more cooperative. Drink a glass of grape juice instead, or chew on an apple.

3. Walk away from the situation before the situation paralyzes you. Is the dog wagging the tail or is the tail wagging the dog? Take a five-minute time out. You don't have to stand in a corner, but it's good just to take a break and find something funny to divert your energy. Shift your focus. Give three people compliments when you're on your break.

4. Take a deep breath. Take *three* deep breaths.

5. Repeat in your mind: *"calm down, calm down."*

Remember, smart people speak from experience. Even smarter people, from experience, don't speak. He who restrains his lips is wise.

Recognizing the Look and Feeling of Negativity

Most of us can feel the negativity building in us before it dominates. This is the time to take action—while it's building, before it dominates. If you are feeling out of control with your emotions, follow the steps just mentioned.

I inherited the **"Look"** from my Irish mom. With one **"Look,"** I have been known to clear a room. The numbers vary, but approximately 55 percent of your message is nonverbal. Practice the old **poker face**, or the Mona Lisa expression. No one knows what cards you're holding in a good gin rummy game when you have perfected the **"Poker Face."** Likewise, no one knows what's in the mind of a good manager who's wearing a nonjudgmental expression on his or her face.

The Attack Stance

The major muscles are affected when negative emotions take over. I asked my workshop audiences to identify the physical changes they feel when they are involved in a negative situation. The first thing they identified was tightness in their neck. And then they identified the tightness in the muscles around the eyes and mouth.

Their fingers make a fist, and the muscles in their arms twitch.

Their breathing almost stops, and their faces turn red.

Fire starts to come out of their already flared nostrils, and their teeth grow. As the hair on the roof of their mouths starts to choke them . . . Aren't we soooo attractive and approachable when we're angry, frustrated, and unable to keep our negative emotions in check?

For most of us, our emotions do not just surprise us. We can feel them coming. And it's at that point that we develop an attitude. This is the time for making responsible choices (because you do have a choice when it comes to attitude). Which attitude will benefit you in the big picture?

Obviously we are not able to control ourselves the minute negative feelings start to kick in. We have to talk ourselves through them. Talking to ourselves is actually a steadfast ritual for most of us—whether you realize it or not. Dr. Joyce Brothers said that highly intelligent people talk to themselves. Ninety-nine percent of the people I interviewed say they talk to themselves. They also admit that about 98 percent of the self-talk is negative. If we talked to strangers and friends as negatively as we talk to ourselves, no one would want to be around us.

𝔍mproving Your Private Conversation

Diplomats are not born; they are made through perseverance and discipline. So, too, it takes perseverance and discipline to redirect the chatter between your ears to positive talk. It is tough because most people are convinced they can't change what they think. But if *you* can't stop what you think, then who can do it for you? Remember, your thoughts are closely related to your actions. "As within, so without." When you think positive thoughts, your actions will be positive.

In the Bible, in Romans 15, under the section entitled "Patience and Self Denial," it says:

> *"We who are strong ought to put up with the failings of the weak and not to please ourselves; let each of us please our neighbor for the good, for building up. For Christ did not please himself; but, as it is written, 'the insults of those who insult you fall upon me.'"*

> *"May the God of endurance and encouragement grant you to think in harmony with one another, in keeping with Jesus Christ, that with one accord, you may with one voice glorify the God and Father of our Lord Jesus Christ."*

This passage calls me to make changes in my thinking instead of continuing to feed the fire of discourse. Once we get over the game of being "one better" or competing with the difficult person, then we can set up a more approachable and solution-oriented experience. Remember the philosophy and wisdom of the Almighty to pursue what leads to peace and to building one another up.

Our inner conversations can be altered as soon as we get the message that we are upset. Fostering harmony in your mind, in your thoughts, will calm you, and well-chosen words will promote harmony in your relationships. Thinking in harmony is an ideal. It means not to think with rigid uniformity, but with consideration of other's views.

> *"When faced with the choice between changing your mind*
> *and proving that there is no need to do so,*
> *almost everyone gets busy on the proof . . ."*
> —*John Kenneth Galbraith*

If you have a plan for getting along with the difficult personalities in your life and a system for dealing with your own negativity, you will be destined to succeed. Like any other area of our lives, while we are planning our time and activities, we really should plan to put one new discipline in the plan. By helping our minds stay focused on positive acceptance rather than on the differences between ourselves and others, we will find that the quality of our relationships improves. Give them a break! And at the same time, give yourself a break too.

July

Glory, Glory Hallelujah, His Truth Is Marching On

*J*uly is a hot month, and it's the middle marker for summer. In my part of the country, Kansas, this is a lazy, hot month.

The numerous activities that were just starting in June are regular parts of our summer schedule now. An issue near and dear to our hearts is our tendency to jam as much as we can into one day—and then feel cross, disappointed, or frustrated when we can't accomplish it all. This month, we are going to eliminate the negativity of overbooking ourselves and learn how to book the really important things into our calendar to enjoy ourselves.

Never forget that the greatest idea at the wrong time is a loser. With real estate, it's location, location, location. With ideas, it's timing, timing, timing. Is the timing right for your new idea? Would it have been easier to do last summer? What opportunities will you miss if you don't do it now?

Time management programs came on the scene during the 1970s, and I was out there pushing them. Now I call it time management in a box. So long as you structure your every minute, you can fit just about everything into the box. This was also a time when mothers entered the workforce in great numbers, full of guilt and attempting the great lie. This lie was that we could have it all without making any sacrifices. We could work outside the home and inside as well. Realistically, we can't wake up much earlier or we'll meet ourselves in the bathroom. I read an article that says if you set your clock 15 minutes earlier you can fit so much more into your day. Not really. I was victim to this whole time management movement and taught it with passion. It does work for a while, helping you to structure your life and discipline your day. But living your life in a box and ignoring your own place in your life's journey brings disenchantment and burnout.

Did your parents ever tell you that there's a time and place for everything? As a kid I did not understand that message as much as I do as an adult. If we take the time and concentrate on the immediate, we can eliminate the job. When I'm done . . . I can go exercise. Basic but true. Another basic and true piece of advice comes from the Bible. This time management program will put life into perspective when your emotions are on a roller coaster ride and you are racing to ten places. It's from Ecclesiastes, verses 3 and 4.

Man Cannot Hit on the Right Time to Act—The Ultimate in Life Management

*There is an appointed time for everything, and a
time for every affair under the heavens.*

*A time to be born, and a time to die: a time to
plant, and a time to uproot the plant.*

*A time to kill, and a time to heal: a time to tear
down and a time to build.*

*A time to weep, and a time to laugh: a time to
mourn, and a time to dance.*

*A time to scatter stones, and a time to gather them:
a time to embrace, and a time to be far from
embraces.*

*A time to seek, and a time to lose: a time to keep
and a time to cast away.*

*A time to rend, and a time to sew: a time to be
silent, and a time to speak.*

*A time to love, and a time to hate: a time of war,
and a time of peace.*

That is your "out of the box" reality time management program for life. Of course, there's nothing wrong with picking up any variety of day planners to remind you of where you're supposed to be.

When we look back at our lives, will we really remember all the busy things we fit into them, or will we remember the times when we could dedicate and commit ourselves to something meaningful? Did we allow ourselves to focus on the time at hand or are we always in the past or the future?

107

Heads Up! How to Use Time for Yourself

1. Go to a farmer's market with a big basket to carry your fresh vegetables and fruits home in.

2. Buy a long loaf of bread, fresh flowers, and something good to put on that bread.

3. Call a friend to go to the market with you—a child, a spouse, or an older person who needs transportation.

4. Make July the month to eat only live foods. Let me make myself clear. A live food is food that comes straight from the ground—freshly picked tomatoes, carrots, and so on. Fresh lean meat and fish. Nothing from a box.

5. Barbecue outdoors every night in July. Enjoy grilled vegetables and meats.

6. Make s'mores. Roast a marshmallow on a stick over hot coals, put it on top of a chocolate bar in a sandwich of graham cracker. Don't forget a good story from a fun memory of when you were a kid.

7. Set time aside to go outdoors and count or catch fireflies.

8. Go fishing. Take an afternoon and have some fun.

9. Listen to the sounds of July—the birds, tree frogs, and crickets sound different from the bird noises of spring.

10. Watch at least six sunsets a week. Acknowledge the creation of God's great Earth.

11. Work in your garden in the evenings when it's cooler.

12. Take long walks—with your dog, with your kids, with someone special.

13. Make homemade ice cream and have an ice cream sundae party.

14. Get to a Fourth of July parade. Wave to everyone and applaud the local kids.

15. Hang your American flag with pride and remember what the colors of the flag stand for, especially the red blood that was shed for our freedom to live in the most incredible country. I have lived in other countries and given seminars in other countries, but my eyes always fill with tears when my plane touches down in the United States of America.

The Perfect Family Vacation

If you have kids, this is the time of year for the family vacation. Maybe yours will be many little trips, or perhaps one longer one. Studies show that the family trip is extremely important. In fact, 75 percent of the people interviewed said it was the most important part of the summer.

Sometimes these trips turn out to be a lot more work than you expect, and no one feels rested. Under normal circumstances, your children have their own routine, just like you do. Kids have their own community with their friends and may resist anything you suggest when it comes to vacation ideas. I vividly recall when my oldest daughter chose to go on a trip with a friend's family rather than with our family. She was at an age when friends were more important than family. How rude, I thought!! But the great thing was that she was growing up.

Heads Up! Planning the Perfect Family Vacation

1. **Have a game plan.** Hold a family meeting where everyone's encouraged to participate. Let everyone know that all ideas for the trip are welcome. Believe it or not, my husband is the biggest baby of all on a trip.

2. **Listen fairly to the ideas.** Remember, your children may not get excited at the thought of sitting in Grandpa's hot, unairconditioned house for a week.

3. **Be democratic.** Make sure everyone is heard. Nearly half of teenagers say they aren't able to talk to their parents because their parents don't listen to them. (Guilty!)

4. **Set a budget.** Vacations can put a strain on the old pocketbook. Be up front about how much you can afford. Remember, you have to eat and pay the mortgage when you get home.

5. **Go with the flow.** Blessed are those who are flexible on a family vacation, for they are rarely bent out of shape. If your teens want to go to the mountains but your little munchkin is wanting to go to the beach, locate a place in the mountains with a lake.

6. **Move around.** Get information from chambers of commerce or your travel club for day trips you can take from your main vacation spot.

7. **Create a vacation grab bag.** Have family members write down something they want to do for a day. Put all the ideas in a jar. Take turns drawing out a new activity for each day. (Don't cop an attitude when your activity isn't chosen.)

8. **Balance your need to rest and relax with your family's need to keep going.** Be understanding and compassionate about each person's situation.

9. **Consider bringing your teenager's best friend with you.** Sure you want this to be "family" time, but maybe that friend doesn't have a special time in his or her life. You might be the model from which that young person builds a future family.

10. **Remember, there's a beginning, middle, and ending to everything.** At the beginning of the trip, have a special place to stop. In the middle, relax. If things don't go as planned, don't sweat it. Take care of things as they happen. And as for the end, it isn't over till it's over. In my mind, that always means when the car is unpacked. So plan something neat before you hit the garage. On the way home, take everyone to a drive-in movie or to a fair you see from the highway. As with any good book, every part of your vacation will be remembered when it's carefully constructed. If it wasn't great, keep your sense of humor. That's life—and you always have next year . . . God willing. (Your kids will all be a year older, and you will be a year wiser.)

August

The Heat Is On

*A*ugust is a month of stifling heat in many parts of the country. But remember, it takes both heat and water to obtain growth.

Our growth is proportional to the lessons and experiences of our lives. A favorite fish of many fisherman is the Japanese carp, known as the koi.

The koi is an interesting fish because if you put it in a small fish bowl, it will grow to be two or three inches long. Place it in a larger tank or small pond and it will reach six to ten inches. When you put it in a large pond, it can get as long as a foot in length. And when placed in a lake where it can really move around, it can be as big as three feet.

Our growth is determined by the size of the world within ourselves. If we choose to remain in the small world we have created, then we can grow only a little, if at all. But if we choose to expand our world, then we will grow and grow. We constantly need to expand who we are so we do not remain who we are. Think of August as the time of year that you will be doing some real growing on the inside and preparing yourself and all those around you for the up and coming season of change.

> *"God only gives me what I can handle. I just wish he did not have so much confidence in me."*
>
> —*Mother Teresa*

Heads Up! Raising the Bar on Your Inner Growth Chart

1. **Spend a few good hours in your favorite bookstore or library.** Did you know that only 3 percent of the population have and use library cards? Go to a section that offers you challenge and diversity.

   If you have lost a friend or are having a tough time in a relationship, then find books on how to improve in this area. Be careful not to get books that defend your side even more. Growth means learning and expanding your scope.

2. **Commit to reading the Bible every day.** The difference between commitment and interest is simple. When you are committed, you accept no excuses, only results. Start from the Old Testament and work up to the New Testament. Get a study guide if the material is dry to you, or you just don't understand what you're reading. The Bible is an amazing book and although there's a copy in many people's homes, it's not opened enough. *That reminds me of a little story I heard about a family who had a minister over for dinner and thought it would be impressive to have him read the Bible. The Mother asked the little boy to go get the Bible, the book Mother and Dad are always reading. The little boy came back with the Sears catalog.*

3. **Learn to control yourself.** One big stress for most people is getting along with different people, both at work and socially. Talking to people even in general can bring on a lot of negativity. Learn some different techniques

from personalities who do this for a living. Watch their different styles on television, or go to a seminar or class. Learning to handle *your* responses and reactions will eliminate a great deal of negativity. Believe it or not, there are times when everyone feels at a loss for the right thing to say. During those times, I try to listen and to relate.

4. **Arm yourself with "reality."** Don't think that negative things can't happen to you. That's how we become vulnerable to feelings of hopelessness. Surround yourself with family, friends, and support groups while things are going well. Negative events often don't happen in isolation; they seem to travel in packs. It never rains one drop at a time.

5. **Know you are loved by more people than you think.** Make a list of all those who love you and really think a lot of you. If your list has even one person on it, then you are loved by at least one other person. Make sure you put God's name on that list. He loves you unconditionally and is certainly waiting for you to recognize it and love Him back.

Turning Up the Heat on Enthusiasm

August is a hot month. I relate "hot" to passion and "passion" to enthusiasm. Let's look at what enthusiasm really is.

It is a fire, a passion within. Real enthusiasm is not something you put on and take off. It is a way of life. We all know people who are enthusiastic. We like being around them. Enthusiastic people usually hang out with others like them and tend to infuse others with enthusiasm. Watch out, an enthusiastic attitude is easier caught than taught.

Like the chicken and the egg, enthusiasm and success seem to go together; I suspect, however, that enthusiasm comes first.

ℋeads 𝒰p! Catching 𝓔nthusiasm

1. Go to a place where you felt enthusiastic before. Think. Was it when you went to an amusement park? Or was it when you went to a special concert? Can you physically get there?

2. What is stopping you from being enthusiastic? Is it sadness from a change of lifestyle, or is it from illness? Dig deep and see what stands between you and your passion for life.

3. Do you get enthusiastic from little things in life, or do you take them for granted? Remember Mercedes Rameriz, the plane crash survivor. Her words of wisdom for us were not to take anything for granted. Enjoy the blue sky, the snow, the heat, and the people you love.

4. Enjoy the moment you are in. When we are waiting for the other shoe to drop all the time, we miss the moment and the enthusiasm we had the opportunity to feel. The "ya, buts," can destroy the moment too often. Make a commitment to stop yourself when you start to say, "Ya, but . . ."

5. If we only see what we no longer have in our lives, we miss out on all we do have. Of course, we all have those dark moods. But when you feel yourself slipping into one, take the time to look at what you have, not just at what you can't have. We don't always get life on our terms. Sometimes we have to expand our terms and get on with life *as it is.* We can either change our attitudes about what we do not have, accept it temporarily, or change it.

"Death is not the greatest loss in life.
The greatest loss is what dies inside us while we live."
—*Dr. Norman Cousins*

New Beginnings

August is the end of summer and a time to uproot the plants of heat and look towards the produce of the cool days ahead. It is not the stopping of growth, but the beginning of a different type of growth. As the old cucumber plants lie wilted in the ground, it is time to be thankful for the fruit you reaped and to clear a spot for a second growth of beans, radishes, pansies, and mums. God offers us a new start at the end of summer and into the transitional season of fall. It is a time to reap and a time to sow, a time to uproot and a time to seed.

Don't throw away the last days of summer in your planning for the fall and winter. Instead, go to the outdoor cafes and parks for as long as possible.

Summary of the Season

The long hot summer . . . it's a tremendous time for outdoor growth and personal inner growth. Relationships formed while camping, traveling, and visiting will renew and grow as we stay in contact throughout the year. Read good books, eat fresh food, and enjoy lazy days. Heat and passion go together—get the passion for life. Burn with the love of the Lord and keep the fires going through the fall and winter months.

> *"I worry that our lives are like soap operas. We can go for months and not tune in to them. Then six months later, we look in and the same stuff is still going on."*
>
> *—Jane Wagner*

Humor Therapy

"After God created the world, He made man and woman. Then, to keep the whole thing from collapsing, He invented humor."
—*G. Mordillo*

There was a man who was caught in a raging flood. A rescuer came in a boat and screamed, "Grab the line buddy, I will get you to safety."

The man yelled back, "Jesus is going to save me."

Then a helicopter came and the pilot yelled, "Grab the line, and I will pull you to safety."

The man yelled back, "Jesus is going to save me."

The man drowned and went to heaven. When he saw Jesus, he said, "Why didn't you save me?"

Jesus replied, "I sent a boat and a helicopter, buddy."

Exercise Therapy

Summer is a great time for any type of exercise. The sport for this season is the greatest aerobic exercise in the world, and that is swimming. The feel of the water is cooling and relaxing, and the workout you get from stretching and using all your muscles is incredible. (And you can't sweat because you're already in the water.) I swam on several teams as a young girl, and the muscles I built back then are still holding my body together. It is an exercise that you can do either in an indoor pool or an outdoor pool, and it will take your mind off your problems.

Start with five laps of the pool without stopping. Then go to ten and twenty. Swim with passion. Use your legs to propel yourself across the pool and pull with your arms like you mean it. Go for it. When you jump or dive into the water, stretch as long as you can. Reach for the other end of the pool and start your kick.

Swimming is a sport you can do alone or with your family. You don't have to wait for a partner. Growing up, I was a pretty good-sized kid. At age 9, I was slamming into doors and tripping over my own feet. My ever-so-wise and worried mother took me to swimming lessons and found this was one place I couldn't hurt myself. So I swam and swam myself into the National Aquatic School and Instructor of Instructors. I still have the skills and have taught, not forced swimming, to all my kids. They all swim for exercise wherever they are, and it is a sport I hope they will pass onto their children.

Spiritual Therapy

We all get very absorbed with our feelings and pressing issues, but I think that my happiest times occur when I am absorbed in other's needs. By forgetting myself, I find my heart and feel my love for others. By doing for others and loving the deeds, I get a much higher level of satisfaction than the normal instant gratification of material goods.

Anyway

People are unreasonable, illogical, and self-centered.

Love them anyway.

If you do good, people will accuse you of selfish, ulterior motives.

Do good anyway.

If you are successful, you win false friends and true enemies.

Succeed anyway.

The good you do will be forgotten tomorrow.

Do good anyway.

Honesty and frankness make you vulnerable.

Be honest and frank anyway.

What you spent years building may be destroyed overnight.

Build anyway.

People really need help but may attack you as you help them.

Help people anyway.

Give the world the best you have and you'll get kicked in the teeth.

Give the world the best you've got anyway.

—From a sign on the wall of Shishu Bhavan,
the children's home in Calcutta

Cooking Therapy

What is summer without good barbecue? I never realized that so many barbecue capitols exist in the United States. When I lived in Texas, there was great Texas barbecue. Then I traveled to Memphis, Tennessee, where I was told I hadn't tried barbecue until I had tried Memphis barbecue. It was great too. Then I moved to Kansas City, and I found out that the city is not only the Jazz Capital of the world but also the Barbecue Capital. As a kid, barbecue meant tossing a hamburger on some coals. You see, Canton, Ohio, is the Football Hall of Fame Capital, but definitely not in the barbecue competition. In Kansas City and many other places, actual competitions are held with great big prizes. People from the state of Washington to the state of Florida who take pride in their barbecue bring their tents, campers, and smokers to the competition sites. Living in Kansas City, I was lucky enough or smart enough to befriend a great competitor who shares his great barbecue with us. I am including one of the winning recipes. I love this stuff. You will agree it is "to die for." Thank you David Wanamaker.

World's Greatest BBQ Chicken
(better than any restaurant)

Ingredients

2 packages BBQ marinade mix (Adolph's for the Grill
Hickory Barbecue)
2-3 lbs. chicken pieces
apple juice
zip-lock bags (gallon size)
dry barbecue rub (Oklahoma Joe's Original BBQ sea-
soning)
several handfuls of hickory wood chips or 3-4 chunks
(dry if using a gas grill; soak in water at least half an
hour before using on a charcoal grill)
medium-sized shallow, aluminum foil pan
spray bottle
charcoal

Wash chicken and pierce deeply in several places with fork, or
with a sharp instrument.

Place the chicken in zip-lock bags. Mix the marinade using
one half water and one half cup of apple juice per package.
Pour over the chicken in the bags.

This process works best if you use a kettle-style charcoal
grill or a gas grill. If you're using a charcoal grill, start 30 to
35 charcoal briquettes. If you're using a gas grill, start your
fire using half your gas burners. Do not cook chicken over
hot coals.

Process

Remove chicken from liquid and cover with dry spices.

Do this to taste . . . it can get hot.

When the briquettes are ready, move half to one side of the grill.

Drain the wood chips and spread a handful over the briquettes on both sides of the grill. This produces great smoke that will add great flavor to your chicken . . . not to mention a great aroma to your hair, face, and neighborhood. (Sorry, Dave, I had to throw that in.)

If you're using a gas grill, wrap your wood chips in foil and puncture the foil several times with a fork. Place them over the hot side of the grill.

Place your aluminum foil pan, filled with hot water, in the center of the grill or charcoal grate. Replace the cooking grate. If you use a gas grill, get a deeper pan and fill it half with water. Then place it over the hot side of the grill.

Place the chicken on the cooking grate where it is not directly over the fire. Close the grill. Fill the spray bottle with apple juice. Spray every 20–30 minutes. Add more wood, if necessary.

The chicken is done when the juices run clear (about 90 minutes).

While you are outdoors waiting for your World's Greatest Chicken to cook, it is a great time to play. You can do a number of things to relieve negativity during this time:

1. Inhale a lot of the chicken aroma.

2. Toss the old Frisbee or yucky tennis ball to your dog or cat.

3. Weed the flower garden.

4. Read the newspaper.

5. Design a new landscape for your back yard.

6. Make a pitcher of iced tea or lemonade and offer some to your starving neighbors.

7. Sit quietly and pray that your chicken recipe is as good as old uncle Dave's.

8. Write little notes to all your kids . . . the ones in your house and the ones away at school.

9. Invite your spouse or best friend (in my case, it's the same person) out to sit and visit.

10. Bring out some music to get your barbecue rolling. Chicken always cooks better to music. (If chickens lay eggs better to music, then maybe it will cook better to music too.)

Fall

A Time of Transition and Thankfulness for All the Graces about Us

Letting go of the bounties of summer and accepting the unknown gifts of autumn takes a tremendous amount of courage. Enjoying every day and the transition each one brings moves us one step closer to winter.

For some people, autumn is a time of year for remorse at the end of all that summer brings; for others, it is a time of preparation for the entrance of winter. The squirrels are playful, but their activities seem to have more purpose than their August rompings over my roof. The blue jays and cardinals stay close to my house because they can count on a big fat bird feeder to feast from during the cold period that lies ahead.

No two months are the same in autumn. September is a season of its own. Beginning in September, you can see the first appearances of change. By October there is no doubt that the cycle of nature is in its glory. November brings the last of the season change. It is a time of cleaning up after the falling of the leaves.

Just as the trees are reluctant to turn loose their leaves, so are many of us reluctant to let the summer go. God has a way of protecting His glorious trees. A tree does not let go of its leaves until the leaves send out a chemical substance that allows the tree to survive the winter's cold. God has a way of protecting us as well. If we but place our trust and faith in Him, he will see us through our times of "letting go."

What exactly are we dealing with in the fall of the year?

1. New schedules, usually with more rather than fewer things to do

2. The loss of the early morning sunshine with the delayed sunrise

3. Shorter days because of the earlier sunset

4. Mood shifts in anticipation of a dark winter

5. Not knowing what weather to expect from morning to evening

For some people, autumn is a time of struggle because they have to let go of their children and friends who are going off to school. For some parents, the big yellow bus represents the passing on of their children to the school systems. From this time on, the little one will be influenced by many strangers. This is truly a large moment for the entire family.

It is an especially challenging time for those who must send their firstborn to a college in another city. It is a mixture of relief that you pulled this parenting thing off and the kid made it into a good school as well as fear that you won't be able to meet the financial demands that a college education entails. As a parent, you know that freshman year is a huge adjustment for your child to the world outside of your home. It is a big adjustment for you too . . . no more waiting up for them to come home, no more taking their phone messages, no more begging them to eat, and no more tired hug when they feel sad.

I drove my number one daughter to a school eight hours from my home. The trip up was filled with loud music, laughing, and anticipation of what college life would be like. She was so excited to get started. Her going to college was a dream for us. It had not been an easy journey, and my daughter certainly did her part to earn scholarship money to help. But when we unpacked all her trunks, placed her possessions in her room, and it was time for me to leave, we both cried and hugged like our hearts were going to break. We were really close, and that part was so hard. She ran down to the end of the drive when I was pulling away. I mustered up a smile, but I could hardly see the road for my tears. I cried the entire trip home. We somehow made it the first couple months, but it was a push for both of us.

This was suffering, but we could do nothing about it. We both realized that you cannot grow if you do not move and change. The following suggestions are things that helped me get through the first autumn without her in my life.

1. Sending creative care packages to school (food, decorations of the season)

2. Finding other moms in the same situation

3. Planning the visit for the Thanksgiving break

4. Weekly phone calls

5. Planning the Parents Weekend visit to school

September
A Season of Its Own

This is a month that starts the noticeable transition, a time to watch once again the Almighty work in action. The leaves turn orange, red, gold, brown, and yellow. Summer gardens just will not let go of their produce. The second planting of beans and radishes are taking on new green leaves, while the zucchini leaves turn gray. Just standing in the middle of the garden gives you the whole picture of the transition taking place. There is the new crop, the birth of new fruits, the still-green tomatoes, and the dried corn stalks standing just as tall but looking so different from the corn-bearing stalks they were. I have summer, winter, spring, and fall right in the corner of my backyard. Much like our own lives, there is a beginning in spring, a growth in the summer, a coming to maturity in the fall. As we go through the middle of our lives, our hair can turn color, maybe many colors, just as autumn's leaves do. The winter of our lives is indeed a time of rest and quiet reflection of all that we have been graced with. We remember the fruits of our labors, the sufferings and the victories.

Take a trip to the local grocery store or farmer's market. Relish the colorful green and orange squashes and gourds. The early pumpkins and the first harvest of apples treat you to new flavors and fragrances. Even the sky on a sunny day in September looks a deeper blue. The smell of the air is different during this transition, not really the smell of dry leaves yet but different from the hot August days we just made it through. The sounds of September are unique too. We leave behind the tree frogs of summer and tune in to the cadence of the crickets.

Autumn is not as subtle as spring when it comes through. It is more brilliant, like a wise, mature God. It shows off its power before it takes a rest during winter.

There is a lesson in all seasons. When God takes away the daylight of the summer, He puts it back in the vibrant color of the fall. Just as when we lose something in our lives, we find that other gifts appear.

The Avoidance of Suffering

Most of us try to avoid the topic of suffering as much as possible.

Suffering is simply having what you do not want and wanting what you do not have. So if you have cancer, you are suffering because you have what you do not want. If someone who is close to you dies, then you are wanting what you do not have. But these are extremes. Most of us have to suffer in the day-to-day "busyness" of running here and there and never feeling appreciated. Our tolerance cup runneth over as we experience the stressors of each day. When I focus on myself too much, I can complicate an ice cream cone. My concern level for what might happen and what I do not want to happen causes me suffering.

When my mother suffered with ovarian cancer more than twenty-five years ago, she never complained. Once she was a beautifully built woman of about 140 pounds, but the illness took her to 90 pounds. Her great faith in the Roman Catholic Church and God did not waver under the test. My mother told me she was suffering so I would not have to suffer with the same cancer. She believed that by her suffering someone would get well.

Pain is a lonely thing, but that doubles when you are suffering someone else's pain. You must help others who are suffering by listening and giving them sympathy and love. Love is the best helper for those who suffer. The love of the Almighty, believed and accepted, will take care of pains. Only our Lord can handle it all. So give it to Him. Lift up your suffering and your remorse for what you cannot have and for what you have that you do not want.

*"Miserable are the persons who do not have
something beyond themselves to search for."*
—*Charles L. Allen*

*"Sweet are the uses of adversity, which, like the toad, ugly
and venomous, wears yet a precious jewel in his head."*
—*William Shakespeare, As You Like It*

Heads Up! Suffering through Suffering

Here are some tips to help you deal with the negativity caused by suffering, whether it is from big events or small ones.

1. Although you do not like suffering, attempt to see what you have at your disposal and not what you do not have at your disposal. Once again, refocusing yourself to someone else's suffering will help you deal with your own situation.

2. Life without suffering would not produce any good songs or stories or lessons. You learn from suffering and you grow stronger. Whenever you build character, you suffer.

Country western singers would not have any material to write about, and we would not be able to identify with sad songs and movies. Just for fun, write your own sad song. Just when you are convinced that the world is beating up on you, marvel at the stories you'll gain from it all.

3. Do you own this misery, or is it someone else's misery you are feeling? If you are the one suffering deeply, you know what needs to be done. If for a time you render yourself unable to cope and carry on, then accept that. It is normal to go on "pause" during great times of suffering. You may need to call in some friends for support, a pastor of your church, or a professional for grief counseling. Sometimes we can handle things better if we have help. Perhaps the lesson in some suffering is that we are not meant to bear it all alone. Going solo usually has more devastating effects than joining hands with someone who will listen and fill in for you. Misery loves company. Get support either in a group, in your church or temple, or on a retreat away from it all.

There is no crime or shame in suffering, whether it is from an addiction, loneliness, or any other of life's events. Sometimes you can wear suffering like a badge because you know you made it through the tough time, even though you may have had your doubts.

Just remember this: Suffering is God's megaphone to get our attention. Jesus was crowned King of Kings because of his suffering, and he saved us all.

When you are carrying someone else's suffering, you are walking with a heavy load. To feel others' pain is not only admirable but saintly. The difficulty with this type of deep loyalty and love is that it is against the popular norm of not taking responsibility for anyone but yourself. According to the popular psychology, we need to let it go and move on. If a problem cannot be fixed within a 30-minute time span, like on a television sitcom, then it is just too difficult to work through. Life is not always about being happy every minute of the day. But it is about serving God first, and the happiness comes from helping others. There are two sides of sadness and suffering, but before you can get to the other side, you must go through the process. That takes the time, which is so hard to give.

The way to carry the suffering of others is to lift their illness, addiction, and misery to the Lord. Be clear as to what you are able to do, and do what you can. If it is a person you know, then call that person on the phone, send cards of encouragement, and if possible help them transfer their energy.

Bears wander to the woods to lick their wounds. But bears are pretty tough and eventually come out of the woods. Humans are connected differently. Getting frustrated because a loved one is pushing you away will not help that person. Do not take these reactions personally. Suffering tends to put many people in a state where they feel helpless and are functioning on their last nerve ending—and it is a raw nerve ending. To do nothing at all is the worst thing you can do for a person who is suffering. Don't go into the woods to lick your wounds when you're rejected by someone who is suffering. Do what you can to elevate their spirit. You will be rewarded, maybe not on this earth, but in eternity.

When T.W.A. Flight 800 blew out of the sky, it hit my heart really hard. I did not know anyone on that flight, but it was the sudden death of so many innocent people just sitting in an airplane seat, vulnerable to whatever happened, that took my breath away. It was not a time for celebration. It was a time of quiet and prayer for all the families and friends and souls of all involved. A true suffering.

The bombing of the Federal Building in Oklahoma hit many hard. The television media reinforced our shock and hurt as the camera captured the human suffering. If we had just read about the incident, perhaps we would not have been so touched, but seeing is believing.

You will not eliminate the event that you are suffering over, but you can acknowledge the process of suffering. Accept the gift of suffering and use your faith to get you through it.

Jesus said, "Come follow me and I will give you rest."

4. Most animals are born ready to run. The mother helps them up and off they go. Sometimes the mother doesn't even have to help them up and off they go. But human babies are born so helpless for a time. Deep inside all of us is a resilience that is tougher than we sometimes realize. Remember, even the tiniest of babies can fight for their lives and put their names on the list of miracle children. They suffered during the fight. No one can convince me that they did not feel the pain of the needles and the fright of all the outside voices and hands. But from birth they reached inside and drew on the ability God gave them to come through their suffering. This resilience is the will to live. We have to have the will to go on and get through the normal ups and downs of earthly life. Maybe as we are sleeping, God whispers in our ear the instructions for how to carry on.

5. Perhaps you are suffering and struggling with a new idea that will change many things in your life. That is often how it happens. Like a row of dominoes, one decision will affect many areas of your life. Think of the labor and the conception of a new life.

"Even the weariest river winds somewhere safe to sea."
—Algernon Charles Swinburne,
The Garden of Prospering

Just when you thought it was going to get cold, the fall can turn itself around and give you Indian summer. I think it is to remind us that when we expect the worst, it can turn around and be pleasant. Suffering is a lot like that—a series of ups and downs.

Some of us are very good storytellers and have been known to exaggerate some of our sufferings. I have a friend who likes to tell me the story of the childbirth of her first son. Each time she tells the story, her suffering gets worse and worse. As the story grows, no one could stand the horror she went through.

My point?

Separate the real story from the drama.

This life is a test.
It is only a test.
Had it been an actual life,
You would have received
Further instructions on
Where to go and what to do!

—Found on a
bulletin board

Yom Kippur and Forgiveness

A most important holy day for my Jewish friends is Yom Kippur. This is a serious time of atonement of the soul. It is a day in September when faithful Jewish families go to the temple and pray all through the day. For some, it is a time of forgiveness for the misdeeds of the past year. The really great thing about this day is that one is not forgiven just by reading prayers and saying they are sorry to God. No, they must go to the person they have wronged and make amends. This takes a lot of courage. But the new year can then begin with a clean slate.

We are always searching for the perfection God wants us to have, but we know there is only one perfect one—God. The rest of us are a bunch of people trying real hard and falling a lot.

A very essential way to eliminate negativity is to forgive yourself and to make amends with those you have wronged.

How Do You Forgive the Unforgivable?

"Eating crow is never pleasant—no matter how much mustard and ketchup you put on it. But usually the sooner you eat it, the less unpleasant it is to the taste!"
—Nido Qubein

When you are the one who was wrong, sometimes it's harder to forgive yourself. But when you do, you'll:

1. Realize you aren't the only person in the whole world who has ever been wrong.

2. Sleep better and eliminate those 3 a.m. restless breaks.

141

3. Feel humble.

4. Find that the pain in your gut goes away and you're able to enjoy your food.

5. Enjoy better health. You will not have a heart attack, stroke, or ulcer, or get the flu as easily.

Forgiving Those Who Have Wronged You

It is normal for you to feel hurt and angry towards someone or something that has caused you to suffer. A person who's stirring up gossip, a loved one who did not keep a commitment, a thief who invaded your sense of security, whoever.

The negative effects are:

1. Social isolation

2. Overeating or not eating

3. Loss of sleep

4. An inability to answer the question "why?"

5. Illness, a rise in your cholesterol level from the stress

6. Tightening of the jaw muscles

7. Cynicism about your faith

8. Inability to concentrate

9. Use of drugs

10. Depression; you hide your light and go to the darkness deep inside yourself

Heads Up! Easy Steps to Forgiveness

1. Perhaps a mental visit to Calvary will help you know about forgiveness. When Jesus suffered and hung on the cross, his last words were, "Forgive them Lord, they know not what they have done."

2. D. A. Battista suggested, **"One of the most lasting pleasures you can experience is the feeling that comes over you when you genuinely forgive an enemy— whether he knows it or not."**

What is this pleasure-producing action called forgiveness?

Forgiveness means to erase, to forego what is due; to wipe the slate clean, to release from a debt, to cancel punishment; to personally accept the price of reconciliation; to give up all claims on one who has hurt you and let go of the emotional consequences of that hurt.

Dr. Paul Faulkner, writing in *Making Things Right,* says forgiveness is similar to looking at an old cut on your body that has become a tough, permanent scar. When the cut was fresh, it festered and was painful. Now that the cut has become a scar, you've forgotten the pain. In fact, you seldom think of it at all. But you can still see the scar. Similarly, it is possible to forget the hurt of past resentments. How? By cutting the line with an attitude of love and good will toward the people who have abused you.

Resentment forces us to "refuel" our wounds, while forgiveness heals the wounds. Healing the wounds brings lasting pleasure.

3. The Bible clearly says, **"Do not let the sun go down on your wrath."**

If you live in Alaska, you will have a long time to forgive because of the midnight sun. But then again, the long dark days follow. So if you don't live in Alaska, get to work.

Remember, the heart's memory takes care of the bad and magnifies the joy.

As within, so without. Do not let those who have caused you suffering keep you down too long. Forgive them. Resolve the situation. Clean it up and empty your trash. When you've unburdened yourself mentally and emotionally in this way, your actions will reflect it.

When storm clouds come, remember this song:

Healer of My Soul

Heal me at evening
Heal me at morning
Heal me at noon
Keeper of my soul
On rough course faring
Help and safeguard my means this night
Keeper of my soul
I am tired of straying and stumbling
Heal my soul from the snare of sin.

October

The Season for Festivals and Garage Sales

Decorations really change around town in October. Some of the places have Halloween decorations up and still others are spruced up for Thanksgiving or Christmas. Transition time even in the retail industry . . . just waiting to remind you . . . Like you forgot.

Fall

Many opportunities for negativity busters this month. Big romantic harvest moons and hay rides. There's also still plenty of outside work to keep you occupied before the first frost.

Heads Up! Time to Park the Broomstick and Enjoy the Brilliance of October

Here are some tips to help you get ready for the approaching cold. Doing some of these things ahead of time will help prevent stress later.

1. Get your furnace checked before you turn it on for the cooler nights.

2. Get that chimney cleaned out so you can have great fires in your fireplace only.

3. Check your car tires. Bald tires don't give you the stop you might need on wet leaves or icy rain.

4. If you're concerned about your health, now is the time to get those flu shots. Some places give them free of charge. (Get one for me because I hate needles.)

5. If you have storm windows, get them out on a Saturday and clean them up.

6. Check on the sales. This is a great time to pick up little gifts for that big event in December.

7. Go to the farmer's market a few last times and buy enough apples to bake, or eat fresh.

8. Plant some tulip and daffodil bulbs. They come up if you put them into the ground according to the directions listed on the bag. (Read the section on Spring for my experience.)

9. Go to a local high school football game. If you're in high school, then support your team.

10. Buy a great novel that will take you through a few rainy days you might have in October.

Shifting Energy from the Weather Report to Projects That Can Give You Long-term Pleasure

There are several projects that you can start no matter what your gender or age. Remember this season is about preparation, and when we are prepared, we will enjoy activities more.

To me a project is something I can't finish within an hour's time. So I have a lot of them. The important thing is to get started on these projects. Remember, motivation without mobilization means only frustration. The minute you take action it all starts.

> *I remember a story that will help you get motivated to get a great project underway. When was the last time you tried to make a 40-foot, 45-ton, untrained, satisfied whale do what you wanted it to do? Probably not lately. In San Francisco a few years ago, a humpback whale known as Humphrey was migrating along the California coast when he made a wrong turn that left him stranded. Humphrey became a national celebrity when he turned into the bay, swam under the Golden Gate Bridge, and navigated 70 miles upriver. Humphrey resisted all attempts to get him back to salt*

water. This went on for three weeks as marine biologists tried to lure him with recorded sounds of feeding humpbacks. Humphrey excited the crowds as he finally responded to a familiar sound and followed his friends into the Pacific. People and whales do things because they want to, not because someone else thinks it is good for them. Motivation results from actions that make you feel good inside. If you help show people the benefit of something and how to accomplish it, they will move mountains to get it.

Heads Up! Project Suggestions That Will Eliminate Negativity

When artist Jasper Johns was asked how to create, he replied, **"It's simple, you just take something and do something to it. Then you do something else to it. Pretty soon, you've got something."**

1. Clean out your garage so you'll have room for the car in the colder weather.

2. Check out the areas of your house where most of the living is done and spruce it up a little. Since the lights are going out early outside, you'll be inside a lot more this time of year. Make it a place you want to be.

3. Visit some of the home improvement stores with a pen and paper. Price your project ideas.

4. Get the facts and make a plan.

5. Give yourself a time span for completing the project. If you don't, you'll never get it off the ground and it will be another good idea gone by the wayside.

6. Convince someone to help you or just keep you company while you're doing the project. Working in isolation is for the birds (I don't think they isolate themselves either). We need companionship. Working together on a project is a lot of fun.

7. Give yourself some atta boys and atta girls. We all need the applause.

8. Give yourself a certain amount of time every night or every week to work on your project. Try to make this uninterrupted time. If you want to watch a football game and you need to finish up your project, then take a television or radio and do two things at once.

9. Don't forget food. Pop some popcorn and get yourself some soda and enjoy your project.

10. Remember to switch from a physical to a mental effort every so often so you won't get burned out before you complete the project.

11. Every so often, you might need to ask for help from someone who has a taller ladder or some expertise. Don't underestimate your friends or neighbors. They are probably just waiting to show off some of their handiwork.

12. Plan a celebration to show off your complicated job. Perhaps a football party or a chili dinner where everyone brings their favorite chili—whatever your heart desires. Just have some fun with it. If you're like me, you were very serious doing the project and it wasn't an easy effort. So here's your chance to get the applause you deserve.

Norman Vincent Peale once said, "Plant the seeds of expectation in your mind; cultivate thoughts that anticipate achievement. Believe in yourself as being capable of overcoming all obstacles and weaknesses."

These are words of encouragement and motivation that will help you get going. Even if you're not able for some reason to physically do a project, you can always supply the smiles and the moral support. Food works too. You can pick up or bake up some goodies for the workers. There's more than one way to participate in this activity before the calendar turns to November.

November

The Official Start of the Holiday Season

"If a man finds himself with bread in both hands, he should exchange one loaf for some flowers of the narcissus, because the loaf feeds the body, but the flowers feed the soul."
—*Muhammad (ca. 600 A.D.)*

Heads Up! Balancing the Mind, Body, and Soul During the Holidays

1. Look somewhere else. Finding new ideas is like prospecting for gold. If you look in the same old places, you'll find tapped out veins. But if you venture off the beaten path, you'll improve your chances of discovering new idea lodes. You can't see the good ideas behind you by looking twice as hard at what's in front of you. Where else can you look for new ideas for balance if the old ideas didn't work for you?

2. What is balance to you? Are you getting frustrated because your friend has more time than you? Are you watching a real role model or an ideal one? My ideal is Martha Stewart. Who is yours?

3. Write down all those good ideas for the holidays— maybe a holiday escape with friends instead of your traditional holiday routine. Maybe you could have a reunion at your place to start a new tradition? When you think 'em, ink 'em."

4. Don't start a diet in November—or ever. Just enjoy everyday in moderation.

5. Use good ideas. **"Don't let your search for the great idea blind you to the merely good idea," advises inventor Bob Metcalfe. Reject everything except for the very best and you'll end up with nothing. A lot of disappointed people have been left standing on the**

street corner waiting for the bus marked 'perfection'," says Donald Kennedy. What are some good ideas to help you balance your increased busyness, loneliness, and weariness?

Making Choices

In a popular television game show, people were chosen from the audience based on the fun costume they wore. When they came into the studio, they would carry signs explaining reasons for the outrageous way they were dressed. It was all done in fun. Anyone who was chosen had to answer a question. If the answer was correct, the person could choose door number one, door number two, or door number three. The contestant was teased with the glamour of a shiny new car or boat or a living room filled with furniture and pictures. Of course behind one door was a pen filled with chickens or pigs. The pressure would be on, and the screaming audience would often affect the contestant's decision. The expectation of going home with a new car and boat or furniture was foremost in the contestant's mind. There was no thought given to the taxes that would have to be paid on the winnings or the way the winnings would affect their lives. It was all very momentary.

The game was a lot of fun to watch, and everyone sitting in their living rooms would make choices too. When we make decisions on how to spend time and money, we are influenced by outside voices and a lot of inside voices too. But the important point here is that it is the consequence you have to live with once you overbook yourself, especially during the holiday season. Don't overpromise and overwhelm yourself with expense and pressure. Sure, it's normal to fit a lot more things into a schedule around this time of year, but something has to give. Be careful. No one is going to die if you cannot be the social butterfly seven days a week.

Rest is important. Doing the extra things with the right amount of time allowed to them will be much more enjoyable.

> *"Eliminate the negative and accent the positive and don't mess with Mr. In-between." As the song says, pick and choose what is positive. What's negative and what's in-between that you don't have time for?*

Choose your path carefully this time of year. Once you choose, your choices will control you.

What affects your decision on how to spend your time?

1. The visions of grandeur promoted on television?

2. Newspaper advertisements?

3. The demands and wants of others? (I did not say *needs* of others.)

4. Guilt for not being everything to everybody? (Super woman and Super man both died.)

5. The expectations of perfection? (If you can define perfection, then you can have it.)

> *I was told the Canadian Northlands experience only two seasons, winter and July. As the back roads begin to thaw, they become muddy and the cars and trucks traveling through the countryside leave deep ruts. The ground freezes hard during the winter months, and the highway ruts become a part of the adventure. A sign before you enter such areas says, "Driver, please choose carefully which rut you drive in, because you'll be in it for the next 20 miles."*

Experience is a great teacher. Look back to last year and consider the results of the choices you made. Use your observations to redesign your plan for this season.

Your subconscious constantly records and stores unrelated data from the outside world. Later, it combines these data into good answers—hunches, we sometimes call them. These hunches can lead you to taking more time for yourself, or more time for others. What hunches do you have about what you would like to experience this year?

Reality and Balance

What seems like an incredibly busy life for some people is a normal life for me. I exclude all my wants and needs on some days. And other days, I don't get to my needs at all.

A balanced day even in busy times should include:

1. Morning prayer and Scripture reading.

2. A 20- to 30-minute walk or exercise of some sort.

3. Food. Don't forget to choke down something filling. It may not always be the most nourishing, but you won't die from a junk food day now and then.

4. Time to look your spouse or significant other in the eye and say, "I love you more today than yesterday."

5. At least one hour with your child (if you are a parent). Love your children, listen to them with all your heart and soothe their fears. Parenting is a gift and work from the Lord.

There are twenty-four hours in a day. If you can't turn off the outside world and intrusions long enough to fit in these simple things, then you desperately need to refocus your current game plan.

Eliminating Negativity through Self-realization

Eliminate the following:

emptiness	alienation
apathy	interpersonal conflicts
crime	dependency
alcoholism	drug addiction
fear	insecurity
resentment	jealousy
mistrust	hostility
guilt	self-pity

Create possibilities for the following:

purposefulness	health
joy	self-motivation
contentment	acceptance
fulfillment	creativity
charity	friendship
forgiveness	love
gratitude	kindness
warmth	trust

What control do you have for enjoying a perfect Thanksgiving holiday?

Remember the theme of this book: "As within, so without." No matter how many outside forces try their best to stop you from having a good holiday, it is still up to you. All joy and pain start behind your eyeballs, even during the holidays.

Heads Up! How to Enjoy the Perfect Thanksgiving Dinner

1. Close your eyes and picture what you would like to see happen on Thanksgiving.

2. If you have lost someone, picture that person at the table. That person can be with you, alive in spirit. Do not pretend you do not miss them. Offer a toast to them. I think your loved one will hear those remembrances.

3. It is one day, a special day, but just one of many. If you have to change tradition for a good reason, be flexible. Flexibility is key, and you will be the example for everyone.

4. Whether you are a host or a guest, be of good cheer. If you are in a bad mood in the morning, then pray it away. God will take away bad moods when you praise Him. Your bad mood just goes away.

5. Invite one person you know of who is either a single parent without family nearby or a single person. My friends always say "no" at first, but when gently pushed a bit, they will join and enjoy. Embrace the opportunity to serve. In serving, you receive a true thanks. If you are alone, go and volunteer to help cook. Share yourself with others. Be thankful you have life.

Fall

This is the last month of the transitional period of fall. The next month is defiantly winter. But for November, you can still use oranges, browns, yellows, and the like for atmosphere. The scents of apples baking and pots of spiced teas are a must this month.

Combating Mood Shifts

In November, days grow shorter and shorter. Mood shifts easily result from the lack of sunshine. But there is help.

Heads Up! Lightening Up on Dark Days

1. Change your music selections. Remember, you become what you focus on, and your music has a big influence.

2. Change your lighting around the house so it puts out more artificial sunlight.

3. Go outside anyway. Don't wait for the sun to open the door for you. Open the door even on cloudy and gray days.

4. Wear bright and cheerful colors instead of gray and blue. We do not have to match the sky. I grew up in Ohio, a place where there are fewer sunny days than in the state of Washington. We did not see the sun for months but survived because we did not know any better.

5. Get videos that will mentally take you to a brighter place, not ones that are dark and violent.

The way you decorate the place where you are staying can make all the difference in the world. I visited a little friend in a hospital ward. The ward was so bright, and the halls were decorated for the season. Even the nurses wore brightly colored jackets—and it *did* make a difference. You could feel the positive morale in what is usually a sad setting around the holidays.

It is not a mystery why some people feel fine even when the clouds appear. And why some people feel emotionally paralyzed when clouds appear. It comes from one little word that can activate both your mind and your body. The word is "action." Those who are successful in overcoming the odds are the ones who take the action. A little action is better then no action at all. The worst thing you can do is nothing at all. If you can't take physical action for one reason or another, then take mental.

The season of autumn is a stimulating time of transition. It is three seasons in one, reflecting the transitions of our own lives.

In this section, we have spoken of tasks to undertake in the preparation for upcoming events. The emotional transitions that will happen as life turns from 78 degrees to a cold freeze must be anticipated. By anticipating any and all types of weather in our lives, we can enjoy and prevent a major fall. By preparing and helping others get prepared for the transitions, we are contributing not only to the season of the year, but to the changing seasons of our own lives. As we contribute, we are changed in innumerable ways by those we help.

Autumn is the high point of the year. It is a great teacher of change, extremes, survival, resilience, diversity—and it is all done for us in living color. It is hard not to see the spiritual dimension with all that we do during autumn. A spiritual state of mind is essential for ending the struggle and uneasiness with life.

Fall

Our own bodies and our own minds can only take us so far, but our spirit and faith can lead us all the way. From minute to minute and season to season, balance is there for us. Keeping a balance in our lives while we are faced with not-so-pleasant events is a challenge. But I have faith in the strength of spirit that we all were graced with at birth. Live each day as you would climb a mountain. An occasional glance toward the top keeps the purpose in mind, but many beautiful scenes can be seen from every part of the slope, just as they can in each of nature's seasons, or the seasons of our own lives. So climb slowly, enjoying each passing moment. If you do, the view from the heavens will be even more rewarding.

Humor Therapy

Nothing hits me in the gizzard,

Like waking up to see a blizzard.

I hear the radiator clank and hiss,

Then turn on the air conditioner to reminisce.

The wind cuts deep with every raw fuss:

How come we prayed for this in August?

Along with all my gardening tips for the four seasons, remember this . . . Faith is what you find in churches, synagogues, and people who buy twenty-five cent seed packets.

Exercise Therapy

With the upcoming holidays—Thanksgiving, Christmas, Hanukkah, and New Year's Eve—we are looking at enjoying a lot of good food. To get ready for the grand slam pigout, we have to do one of two things. Either start increasing our food intake by 3,000 calories a day or increase our exercise.

I would rather increase my calories, but my family would rather not see me blow up every year. Here are some exercises I recommend.

1. Increase the strength in your arms so you can lift the fork and spoon easier. Take two 5-pound weights or even a couple of soup cans, and do several repetitions of arm lifts. Extend your arms, palms up, and bend them at the elbow five times. Do this for each arm individually three times. Then extend your arms with the palms down; keeping them straight, lift the arm shoulder height the same number of times.

   I am working on my grandma arms—the really soft and big inside of the arms to hug my grandchildren that my daughters have not delivered yet. I believe that when they are totally loose, then the girls will consider having kids for me to hug. Meanwhile, I hug everyone else's grandchildren and children. But if you do not want the ol' "grandma arms," then bring those weights together. Bend your arms with the knuckles facing each other, and move your elbows in and out. Do not get carried away and go past your shoulders. It is gross when you pop one of those joints out.

2. The next area you need to ready for the "pigout" is the tummy. Mine is past tummy stage, more of a gut. Get down on the floor and do a lot of sit ups—gut busters, I call them. If you have a lot of extra money, then you can send for one of the famous gut buster machines.

Keep in mind, however, that studies show it's not the machine that tones the muscles—it's the action we take with the machine. Working out tummy muscles makes your digestive track stronger for all the junk you'll be putting into it. And if you get it flat before the holidays, then you'll notice when you eat too much because it will stick out. On the count of three, put down this book, lie flat on the floor and do ten sit ups. Do them for at least the length of a short song on the radio. Please be careful not to lift with your back—lift with your stomach muscles.

Spiritual Therapy

I am a professional pray person. I love to pray. When I am walking, I pray. When I have a free minute, I pray. Before I close my eyes and when they open again, I pray. God is about sick of me by now. I suspect that I will be Earth-bound for a long time because I am the last person He wants to bring to heaven.

I have received a beautiful Thanksgiving prayer from the Edmundite missions in Alabama:

There is no home so bleak and bare.

But heaven has sent some blessings there.

No table ever so sparsely spread.

But that a grace should there be said.

No life but knows some moment blest

Of sweet contentment and of rest.

No heart so cold but heaven above

Has touched it with the warmth of love.

So count your blessings, one by one,

At early morn and set of sun,

And like an incense, to the skies

Your prayers of thankfulness shall rise.

Look for the love that heaven sends,

The good that every soul intends.

Thus you will learn the only way

To keep a true Thanksgiving Day.

Live your life as though it were a prayer. Live your life as though you had only a year left. It is, after all, as short as summer vacation.

Serenity

Courage to survive the negativity.

Courage to grow through the negative events.

Courage to challenge your negativity.

Courage to do it anyhow.

Cooking Therapy

Fall is a season with a variety of sounds, smells, and colors. It is also a great time for sports enthusiasts. I must admit, the game itself (football) doesn't make or break my mood, but the anticipation of the game and the food around tailgating or in-home "table-gating," is terrific. The longer the food simmers and fills my home with fragrance, the better the game is. Fall is a state of mind, and I want to close my offerings to you with one of my favorite fall soup recipes. This soup will make you want to go outdoors, just so the aroma will hit you when you enter your warm home.

Christine's Corny Chowder

With a few alterations, this can be made for those very healthy vegetarians. It is great.

Atmosphere: This recipe is all-American, so go for the John Philip Sousa marches. They are great to inspire the mood of the season. You will feel like a Big Ten champ just making this one.

What to wear! A favorite team sweatshirt and a very comfortable and ugly pair of sweat pants.

Ingredients:

1/2 cup unsalted butter
2 medium unpeeled potatoes, diced
1 medium zucchini, diced
2/3 cup onion
2/3 cup frozen whole-kernel corn
1/2 cup Italian parsley
6 cups broth, either vegetable broth or vegetable packets
1 can cream-style corn
1-1/2 cups cream or half-and-half

(If you are making this vegetarian, use fake butter and rice milk instead of the cream and butter. Thicken your soup with corn starch and cold water and add to the pot of soup.)

This is definitely the type of soup you want to share, so before you start chopping, pick up the phone and call someone who hasn't had a good homemade bowl of soup in awhile. This could be someone who lives around you and is living alone, or someone who is just as fun as you are. Even a bowl of chowder can be an event.

1. In a kettle, melt the butter on low. Do not burn it, just melt it. Add the potatoes, onion, whole-kernel corn, and zucchini. Stir the vegetables until they are tender. Add the flour and parsley.

2. Make sure you cut yourself a few raw zucchini sticks—it is a treat. Don't forget to inhale the aroma of all the fresh and healthy vegetables in your kitchen.

    Remember the majorettes from your high school who could toss a baton into the air and turn around and catch it? Now is your chance! No one is looking and you have the marching music on, so get out your wooden spoons and toss away. If you want to blow a whistle as you throw the spoons in the air, it adds more to the effect.

3. Now put the vegetable broth and some salt into your mixture. Add the creamed-style corn. Stir it until it gets bubbly and thick. Let it cook slowly for about 10 minutes, but do not leave it alone too long.

Shazam! You have the best chowder cooking, and it was so easy. This can go in a warm thermos for the stadium or for lunch later.

"Man cannot live on soup alone," says Christine, so we need to add something else to go with this great recipe. My best suggestion is some warm rolls. Either use the kind from the easy-open can, found in your dairy section, or make your own biscuits. Again, the smell of the simmering chowder and the smell of the warm bread will put everyone in a great mood. And why not? The cook has been marching around the kitchen, chopping and dicing until the team comes home.

You have done it. Yes, you have completed the most beautiful soup to look at, the most comforting texture of creamy smooth liquid to sip, the mouth-watering aroma of simmering scents and cozy bread, and of course the soul-stirring sound of the marching bands.

Now it is time for you, the chef, to sit by the fireplace and give yourself at least a 20-minute break. Toss a cloth on the table and have a great time. A great pot of soup will cure whatever ails you and give you a "warm fuzzy." You may not be able to stop the motion of negative situations, but you can take comfort in nourishing your body, soul, and spirit.

How to Help
Teens Cope
with Negativity

The teenage years have been called the summer of our lives. But they are also emotional, hormonal years, and teenagers need help combating the negative aspects that come with them: pimples, puberty, popularity, school, and pleasing parents are just the beginning. Our generation was never thirteen like today's thirteen-year-olds. Today's teens face relocation, conflicting messages from our culture, victimization, illiteracy, family conflict, employment, and their stressed parents. We are pushing them at the breakneck speed of a runaway train.

This section is devoted to the hope that adults, parents, singles, senior citizens, and youth leaders will give some thought to encouraging teenagers to take the high road. That is not always the "fly" way to be. Fly, meaning "really cool." So here's to those great kids out there who have no idea just how great they are. It doesn't matter what color their skin, hair, or fingernails are. It doesn't matter what their body shape is. My part in the scheme is to infect as many teenagers with the tools they need to walk the minefields without getting their legs knocked off.

Our Greatest National Resource

Every school morning, some 42 million American teenagers gulp their breakfast, grab their books, slam the front door, and dash off to school. Among them go not one, but several future presidents of the United States, a handful of future Supreme Court justices, and a dozen future Cabinet members. The greatest natural resource our country has is our children. Parents, teachers, and youth ministers have an opportunity to affect the future of our society by helping teenagers eliminate the negativity from their lives.

Young men between the ages of 15 and 24 account for more than 20 percent of the 23,000 male suicides a year. Young women of the same age are responsible for 11 percent of the almost 7,000 female suicides. It is easy to look at these figures and think that this only happens to families who are split and not paying attention to their teenagers' lives. Or maybe we can accept this information easier if we think that these are the kids who did not have family dinners, churches, or friends to turn to.

Wrong, wrong, wrong . . . no matter what their background, a teenager may be contemplating his or her own death while sitting next to you in church. Suicide never makes sense to those left behind. But maybe we can help troubled teens see the light at the end of the tunnel before the inevitable challenges of these years lead to the terrible permanent choice of suicide.

Teens Are People Too

The following is a list of things teens want most from their life:

1. Happiness

2. Long enjoyable life

3. Marriage/family

4. Financial success

5. Religious satisfaction

6. Love

7. Personal success

8. Personal contribution to society

9. Friends

The interesting thing about this list is that it has the same components that adults from nearly all my audiences tell me they want. Teenagers are not any different in their wants—they just need to mature and the order is different.

A very disturbing fact in the 90s is the reality that our teenagers are the number one target for crime and violence. The music is a response of the culture adults have handed to the teens. And the gap between adults' respect for teenagers and teenagers' respect for adults seems to be holding at an all-time low. The following is some food for thought, more fiber for you to digest, in the hopes that it will raise your awareness of what is going on with our kids. The media would like us to think that young people today are all bad; however, I leave it to you to make your own decisions and communicate with as many as you can. When you're in line for a hamburger, compliment one about their jacket, for example.

How can we help our kids and our grandkids, and in doing so pave the way for a better future for everyone?

First, we must discontinue, as parents and youth leaders, sabotaging our teenagers in these ways:

1. Talking and writing negatively about teenagers as though they don't have feelings.

2. Lumping them into one group and labeling them (i.e., Generation X or some other insulting slang).

3. Separating the family unit through divorce and separation. Contrary to the popular statements "they are young and will get over it," or "children are tough—they don't care so long as they have a place to sleep," teenagers are affected by family upheavals.

4. Giving our teenagers too much information about serious problems that have no known solution. It helps if a young person isn't dropped off the cliff head first.

5. Treating our young people as though they are expendable. Often when they present a problem that is inconvenient to us, we send them off to get "straightened out." We send them away because it's better for them, we tell ourselves. But no matter what our situation or age, we are all children of God. And as God's children, we have the same needs: to feel significant, to have certainty, to have variety, to experience growth in responsibility, to contribute to the family, and to be loved.

When teenagers commit suicide, we know they made a wrong choice. But it does not have to be the final turn of their life. There is so much more road ahead of them. There is a solution to every problem, and suicide is not the answer.

Heads Up! How to Be a Positive Presence in Your Teen's Life

1. Cultivate optimism by committing yourself to a cause, a plan, or a value system.

2. Walk your talk. There can be no happiness if the things we believe in are different from the things we do.

3. Don't compromise yourself. You're all you've got. When your teenager sees you make a stand, he or she will too.

4. You may be the only Bible they read. Represent the Word with honor.

5. Clarify your own values. It is essential for you to experience a richer, fuller, quality life. When you're confused, your teenager loses confidence.

6. Connect your teenager with a different environment. Studies show that teenagers who go back to a negative environment of friends and peers will go back to old patterns. Find a youth group in your area. Most of the church or temple-affiliated groups are run by volunteers and paid staffers who dedicate their lives to the mission of helping young people.

I want to acknowledge all youth ministers and all the time they devote to our kids. A special acknowledgment is for my favorite, Reverend Michael Knight. He is young man who has dedicated about fifteen years of his life to teenagers who want to change their lives. He accepts no excuses for not attending the services. He evens sends buses to pick up kids who don't have transportation to the meetings.

Gangs, drugs, you name it and he will get in its ugly face and shake it from these fantastic teenagers. He truly loves every one of them. Michael has a staff present at the rallies and meetings who have firm and fair expectations for behavior. Michael is loud . . . makes your ears bleed sometimes . . . he is shocking and tells it like it is. He is accountable and has an unconditional love and acceptance for all who walk through his door. Reverend Mike, as they lovingly call him, is a mix of John the Baptist and Simon Peter . . . the Rock. And his group is rightly named Rock Solid.

Take your teenagers to one of these organizations and take them back again. They will want to go back. **And to you, Reverend Mike, you get them and keep on getting them. All our prayers are with you.**

7. Pray for your children. Give them to the Almighty.

8. Pray for yourself so you will have strength.

9. Connect with wise older parents and grandparents to give you advice. The larger the family, the greater the advice pool you have to benefit from.

Confucius, the Chinese philosopher who lived in the fifth century B.C., wrote many maxims. He said the rule of life is to be found within yourself. Ask yourself constantly: "What is the right thing to do? Beware of doing that which you are likely, sooner or later, to repent of having done." Teenagers have within themselves the rules of life, their values. Rather than waiting for someone evil to offer wrong direction, help with the principles and values through the way you live. Values are the glue that hold life's details in place. Peace, harmony, and direction grow in people who know what they value in life.

Heads Up! Helping Teens Make It through the Tunnel of Doubt

When negativity attacks your young kids, it is the worst of times and they do not see the best of times on the other side.

1. Exercising vision is developing an understanding of where you are and where you are headed—you may be the only light they have.

2. Encourage them to talk about the world of tomorrow and develop their vision of it today. It gives them a goal to work toward.

3. Teenagers are very aware of right and wrong. Be the moral irritation in their lives.

4. Vision is not having a plan, but having a mind that always plans. Listen to the plans of your teen and help him or her develop the steps to carry it out.

5. Wake your teen up to the personal power he or she has over any situation. Remember, "as within, so without." They may not be able to exercise control over the situation, but they *can* control their response to it. Don't let them stay in the victim mode long. Empower them with information, options, and love.

Separate Fact from Fiction

Teens aren't being picked out . . . it happens to all of us.

Fact: Your teen will have "those days." Ours is an equal opportunity life plan—no one escapes.

Fiction: Teens have to be victims of society, the establishment, and their friends.

Fact: Teens will go through a few thousand relationships before they find the "one." Some will love them back, some will reject them, and some will not let them go easily.

Fiction: Love is like the movies . . . love at first sight will lead them to the altar of life.

What Today's Teens Think About

While putting together this section, I did a great deal of research. Of course, it wasn't scientific, but what I found out provides insight into the feelings and concerns of a wide cross-section of today's youth. First, I prepared a questionnaire for teens. In addition, I peeked on the bulletin board of life, on the "inner" net, so to speak. I also visited some great conferences for youth minister trainers, and listened like never before to what my own teenager and her friends were telling me.

The following are the questions and answers of the 200 teenagers, aged 13 to 19, surveyed. The study was random and crossed both suburbia and the inner city. It hit the kids from all backgrounds, from the punk group to kids in the Rock Solid Christian youth group in Kansas.

1. Do you ever wake up in the morning and feel really helpless and negative? Is there a real reason for this feeling?

   Answer: 100 percent said they wake up feeling negative and uneasy and don't really know why.

2. Do you feel significant with your family and friends?

   Answer: 60 percent said yes, 30 percent said no, and the remaining 10 percent said they felt *too* significant.

3. Do you go to church on a regular basis?

   Answer: 75 percent said they go, and 25 percent said they did not go.

4. What do you do to release the negative feelings you have?

Answer: 95 percent said they screamed and cried; 5 percent found comfort in their music and reading. A few go to the Bible for peace.

5. If you get rejected by someone you love, how long do you feel the pain?

Answer: 90 percent said they hurt a long time after losing a loved one in a relationship. 10 percent said they were afraid to fall in love and get hurt, that it's better to hide out.

6. Where is your pressure coming from?

Answer: 50 percent said the pressure was from pot, 30 percent from sex, 10 percent from grades, and 10 percent from money.

7. Is it easier for you to love or be loved?

Answer: 95 percent said it was easier to love than to be loved; 5 percent said the opposite.

8. Do your parents support the fact you are going through ups and downs?

Answer: 80 percent said no; only 20 percent felt their parents understood what they are up against.

9. Do you share with your parents what is going on, or are you handling it all yourself?

Answer: 98 percent said they are handling their pressure themselves; only 2 percent share it with their parents.

10. What will bring you peace and joy in your day-to-day life?

Answer: 60 percent said that the love of the Lord gives them peace and joy; 20 percent said being left alone; and 20 percent said that being successful and having money would help.

Amazing what these responses reveal. An overwhelming percentage of youth say they feel helpless and negative, yet only a minority feel supported through their ups and downs. What can we as parents and concerned adults do to offer that support? For one thing, we can help them in the area they say brings them the most peace and joy—the love of the Lord. Young people are interested in prayer and the power of the Lord.

Heads Up! Where to Position Teenagers for Positive Focus

1. Sit with them at your church or temple.

2. At least once a month or more, take them to a youth rally or retreat. These offer nourishment to the soul.

3. Create a peaceful place in your home for scripture reading and prayerful thought.

4. Listen to their doubts and questions, without attacking their beliefs.

5. Walk your talk. Keeping your actions congruent with your words makes it easy for your teen to model you. If you ask your children to behave a certain way and you act the opposite, they will be suspicious.

How to Say "No" without Ruining Your Relationship

Listen to what they are saying, heads and ears up. Observe what is racing through your mind as you're trying to listen to their request; quiet your mind. What are you communicating nonverbally while you are listening? When your teen finishes, acknowledge that you heard what was said. Stay relaxed as you listen. Finally, respond to your child's request.

This is not the time to bring up ancient history. Very simply, remember the golden rule. If you listened to their request and did not interrupt the conversation with one insult, you did a great job. Now it's your turn to reply. Sometimes we resist using that two-letter word because we don't want confrontation. But as crazy as it may seem, teenagers are counting on you to say "no." They also find security in the consequences they have to sow when they cross the line. Young people can only respect authority when they are certain of the rules. Have you heard this before: "Kathy's mom will let her do anything. Even if she's grounded, her mom will let her go to the concerts." Surprisingly enough, teenagers don't respect adults who don't enforce consequences. Make sure your "no" response is clear and definite. There should be no question in your approach.

Heads Up! Saying "No" Meaningfully

1. **Listen to the request.** Respond with empathy. (Nickie, you are really excited about going to France with the school.)

2. **Decline.** (It's something for the future, but not in the plan for this year.)

3. **Give reasons.** (I love you too much to turn you loose in France at 15, and I don't have an extra $2,000 on hand.)

4. **Give some alternatives.** (I will rent you a vacation video on France and cook you a French dinner, or let's plan for this trip your senior year and start making a financial plan where you put some of your money aside and I will chip in some of ours.)

5. **Treat them as though they are smart and thinking young adults**—which is what they are.

Remember, how you handle and stick to your "no's" is closely related to how much your teens feel connected and loved.

How to Help Young People Deal with Failure

A well-adjusted person is one who makes the same mistake twice without getting nervous. There are two benefits to failure. First, when you fail, you learn what doesn't work. Second, the failure gives you an opportunity to try a new approach. Failure is an event; it does not have to be your entire life.

Teenagers are trying very hard to compete within a very competitive world. If they don't feel they are pleasing you and others, they will drop out of the competition.

Failure, in a sense, is the highway to success, because every discovery of what is false leads us to seek what is true. Failure can come in the form of a rejection slip in a romantic relationship or being cut from a sports team. These occurrences obsess teenagers to the point that they lose sleep and don't eat properly. In some, the will to go on is permanently knocked out.

Heads Up! How to Help Teens Cope with Failure

1. **Listen to what they are telling you.** They will tell you how they feel. Failure is real to them. Acknowledge it.

2. **Keep failure in perspective.** The freedom to fail prepares people for the opportunity to succeed.

3. **Point out your teen's significance to the family and in the big picture.** During the teenage years, it is difficult to see life in the

190

big picture. They often see no way out of a situation, and beat themselves up over and over.

4. **Exchange the failure tape with some success tapes.** When a football team loses a game, the coach takes them back to the locker room to view game tapes and see their mistakes. Then they look at tapes of games they won and how they won and why they won. Remember the 10-90 theory. Let your team have 10 percent of the problem and guide them into the 90 percent solution.

Be fair in the time it takes to get up from the fall. Don't make the situation insignificant, but don't overdramatize it either. Share a few of your own failures. Let your teen know how you eventually got up.

Stacy Allison wasn't pleased with failing at her first attempt to climb Mount Everest. She admits to initially experiencing acute disappointment and discouragement. But failure ultimately became her inspiration. "I had to fail to realize that self-worth isn't built upon one accomplishment," she told the *Christian Science Monitor.* It is built through years of setting goals and reaching them. A year later Allison successfully reached the summit and stood on top of the world.

Looking for Love in All the Wrong Places

The relationship parents have with one another is a measuring stick for what your teenager will tolerate in the dating game. A lack of hugs and affection in the home affects young girls, especially. They begin to look outside the family for acceptance. There are far too many abuse stories in dating situations. Physical horse play is one thing, but physical dominance and abuse is another. This is a talk you probably never thought you would have to have with those darling babies you brought home in bassinets.

Heads Up! Talking with Your Teenager about Physical Abuse

1. Take your teen to a good restaurant or a favorite outdoor setting and have a heart-to-heart talk about what love means.

2. Use the scripture as your guide and let them know what the line is between acceptable and unacceptable behavior.

3. Create a safe space for them to talk to you without losing your temper.

4. Take action to protect your teenager. They only know what they see on television. You can do it without putting them in jeopardy.

5. Love your teen and instill self-worth. Let your child know how precious their life is to the Lord and to you. They need to know how they are loved. Stop assuming they know. When the outside world is cold and hurtful, they really have to have love from their home.

Many relationships aren't perfect. Teenagers need to know that every argument isn't going to escalate into a divorce situation. Be careful not to use your teenager as a best friend; he or she may be as tall as you, but your teen's security comes from you. If you're frustrated with your spouse, let your child know that you will work it out as adults. The last thing they need to feel is that they must choose between or take sides with parents. You, as an adult, may need counseling, or simply a walk in the park with your spouse. If you share every little grievance with your teens, they hang onto this a lot longer than you do.

Dads, you are the measuring stick for your daughters' relationships. Any man they date and consider in their lives will be measured to your choices in morals, values, and ethics.

Moms, the mood you set in the house on a day-to-day basis and the relationship of respect you have for your mate will be the model your daughter will acquire and the woman your son will choose.

Don't kid yourself. Your teens are watching and listening.

Parenting teenagers is a challenge. Setting expectations for your children is good, but setting the bar too high and putting conditions on your love will drive them away. Even though you will sometimes want to check their blood type, they really are yours. And sooner or later, maybe when they have their first child themselves, you will finally recognize the payoff of all the work and love you put into those years. Studies show that a mother's self-esteem goes up many points when the last child leaves the nest.

It is up to you to choose how much rope you will give them to experience and learn from life. We all learn from our mistakes, and as parents we do need to let our teens make some. At the same time, we need to physically stand in their way of certain issues such as drugs.

Be there for your teen. Have fun. Teens are people too.
Love them all—green hair, black fingernails, and all.

Fact is, you do have the ability to create what you want even from negative events in your life. Whatever your belief, you are not traveling solo in this lifetime. Reframe not only your mind but your actions, and get moving. Different places and different faces can help begin a new and promising tomorrow.

Discover the keys to fun therapy to dramatically improve your walk through the minefield of life. You will never look at the God-given seasons the same again, and you will call it the nicest thing you have done for yourself.

To contact the author, write:

Christine Rossi
7325 Quivira Rd.
Suite #233
Shawnee, KS 66216-3570

Order Form

YES! I want _____ copies of *Heads Up! A Zillion Ways to Survive Negativity in Your Life* at $16.95* each, plus $4.00 shipping and handling per book. ISBN #0-7872-3533-4

Call 1-800-228-0810 to order by telephone or Fax 1-800-772-9165. Prepayment is required.

❏ Check enclosed
❏ Charge my account:

❏ Master Card ❏ American Express ❏ Visa
MC Bank # ⊔⊔⊔⊔⊔ Exp. Date __/__
Account # ⊔⊔⊔⊔⊔⊔⊔⊔⊔⊔⊔⊔⊔⊔⊔⊔⊔
Signature _____
(required for all charges)

Name _____

Phone _____

Address _____

_____

City/State/Zip _____

Please make check payable to:

Kendall/Hunt Publishing Company
4050 Westmark Drive
P.O. Box 1840
Dubuque, Iowa 52004-1840

Price subject to change at any time.